VENICE: THE ENCHANTED MIRROR

A BEDSIDE COMPANION

Alain Buisine

TRANSLATED FROM THE FRENCH BY

ELFREDA POWELL

Originally published by Editions Zulma 1998
under the title of *Dictionnaire amoureux et savant des couleurs de Venise*

First published in Great Britain in 2005
by Souvenir Press
43 Great Russell St, London WC1B 3PD

French edition © Zulma 1998
English translation © Souvenir Press and Elfreda Powell 2005

ISBN 0 285 63717 7

Typeset by FiSH Books, London
Printed and bound in Great Britain by
MPG Books Ltd, Bodmin, Cornwall

For the first violinist in the
Lavena orchestra

As long as fragments of beauty exist, we can still understand something of the world. As they gradually disappear, so the mind loses its ability to comprehend and to dominate. But because some of its beauty remains, this great shipwrecked ruin that bears the ancient name of Italy still manages to influence the way the world thinks.

Guido Ceronetti (*A Journey in Italy*)

I've visited Venice many times, always in company. I would not come here on my own. This is not a city for interior monologue. All those people who have written so many reams of desolate prose about Venice's wealth of stability and harmony were offloading their dread of introducing funereal symbolism into the Lagoon. And there was no one to tell this melancholy, over-literary bourgeois collection of people that they were hoodwinking us by refusing to acknowledge the traces of rot and death in these waters.

Christian Guidlcelli (*Neighbourhoods of Italy*)

Contents

Contents

∞ Venice: Capital of colour ∞

Great was my joy when I discovered that the first important thesis on the rainbow, the first real attempt to explain this atmospheric phenomenon as light reflecting through raindrops, was actually published in Venice. In 1611, Marco Antonio De Dominis, archbishop of Spalato, who would die in 1624 in the prisons of the Inquisition in Rome, published his *De radiis visus et lucis in vitris, perspectivis et iride tractatus* – *Treatise on the rays of sight and light in lenses and the rainbow*. In this he showed that a ray of light, which is white when it reaches the droplets of water in a curtain of rain, is, as it leaves, broken down into its constituent colours, because the colours that make up white light are susceptible to refraction in different ways. So we have a solar spectrum, the colours of which are – beginning at its lowest point – violet, indigo, blue, green, yellow, orange, red. Even after visiting Venice so many times, I have still never seen a rainbow above the great mirror of the Lagoon, but I console myself with the thought that this chromatic phenomenon would, in any case, be redundant and of little value here, since, for century upon century, the Venetians' sole ambition has been to surround themselves with colour and make us worship it in every possible form and state.

When you descend from the train at Santa Lucia, you get an immediate inkling that Venice, which has many visual treats in store, is out to impress you. For the horrible station was built on the exact site of the old church of Santa Lucia, destroyed in the middle of the nineteenth century, where the corpse of this Sicilian saint was always invoked to cure diseases of the eye (and, also, elsewhere in Italy, to 'blind' deceitful husbands). The legend goes that Saint Lucia tore out her own eyes to send to her betrothed, to demonstrate to him, with supporting evidence, that she intended to devote herself exclusively to God, but the compassionate Virgin gave her back an even more beautiful pair... When the church was demolished in the 1860s, great care and all due solemnity were taken to transport her miraculously preserved remains to the church of San Geremia, rebuilt in the eighteenth century by Carlo Corbellini, where you can still see her today on the left hand side of the sanctuary, wrapped in sumptuous red brocade and protected by a reliquary encrusted with wood carvings and gilt ornamentation. The artfully placed lighting highlights the silver mask covering her face in its glass sarcophagus. And, until a few years ago, two offertory boxes bore the legend (in several languages) 'Santa Lucia, protect our eyes'. To prove that one can have every confidence in this so well-named saint, until quite recently there were on display, all over the glass reliquary, a great many dusty pairs of spectacles, from cheap spindly economy frames to large opulent butterfly models, each duly accompanied by a framed handwritten letter in which their ancient wearers piously thanked the Syracusian saint for having intervened on their behalf... The Church, always believing that modernisation will assure its future, thought a spring clean might be a good idea and cleared away this shambles of popular piety, leaving only a few astonishing silver ex-votos in the display cases, in the form of pairs of eyes (and jettisoning – to no small advantage – most of the stock: you can purchase one of these ex-votos at an antique shop just behind the Guggenheim Foundation for around 90 euros).

Massive and sombre, and heavily inspired by La Salute, the church of San Geremia contains no particularly extraordinary work of art, but when I arrive in Venice I like to linger there briefly, just for the view, on my way from the station to the centre of town. How can I show more clearly that, here, the visual reigns supreme. It was a Venetian Servite monk, Fra Paolo Sarpi, a reputed anatomist who discovered how the circulation of blood worked and who was a specialist in optics, helping Galileo to construct his telescope, who made the first serious analysis of the contraction of the iris at the turning point of the sixteenth and seventeenth centuries.

'Venice is constructed in colour, in light,' Henri de Régnier wrote in *L'Altana ou la Vie vénitienne* (*The Roof Terrace or Venetian Life*). It is 'a colour, rather than a linear, organisation', Adrian Stokes added sombrely in his *Venice*. In fact one hardly dare mention that, almost by definition, Venice was the capital of colour while Florence favoured line and drawing. Giorgio Vasari, principal mouthpiece of the Tuscan tradition in the sixteenth century and greatest defender of *disegno's* theoretical and practical primacy, rebuked Giorgione for renouncing the healthy tradition of preparing a painted composition with drawings on paper. According to Vasari, Giorgione, who worked directly on canvas and brushed in all the shapes without even the smallest of preliminary sketches, thought that 'painting simply with colours was the truest and best fashion of painting and *il vero disegno*'. What a scandal and what a contradiction for the Florentine, who considered that Giorgione was simply 'hid[ing] under the allure of colour his incapacity to draw, as for many years did the Venetian painters'. La Serenissima's artists were irresponsible, heretical even, and, without *buon disegno*, incapable of mastering composition, proportion and anatomy, of ennobling nature by bypassing appearances and attaining the ideal. According to Vasari's aesthetics, 'the quality of its drawing provides the critical measure of a painting, and the significant criteria of formal judgment . . . are basically graphic and plastic values: line and shading, form and proportion. The painter's primary problem is the presentation of the human figure in contour and modelling and to that task colour can contribute only superficially to the basic design' (David Rosand, *Painting in*

Sixteenth-Century Venice). From the Cinquecento onwards it was precisely from these theoretical strictures that Venetian painting escaped, because its origins grew from the convergence of two specific technical factors that became necessary because frescoes deteriorated rapidly in the Venetian climate, and were remorselessly eaten away by damp and salinity from the Lagoon: the two new factors were their use of oil as a medium and canvas as a support. What is more, in Venice, they painted directly with colour: 'certainly colouring is of such importance and power, that when the painter imitates well the natural teints and softness of the flesh, and adds the propriety of the several parts, his paintings seem alive, and as if nothing but breath was wanting', Lodovico Dolce wrote in 1557 in his famous *Dialogo di Pittura intitiolato Aretino (Aretin: Dialogue on Painting)*, which responds vigorously to Vasari's acerbic criticisms. Venetian painting is of value not so much for its subject matter and its graphic quality as for the undeniable supremacy of its colouring. 'Our local painting', one of the characters in Jean Thuillier's *Campo Morto* (perhaps the most beautiful Venetian novel ever written) remarks, 'is characterised by a sensuality that is translated through the primacy of colour over draughtsmanship.' And so he advises Enzo Carmini, the clever forger who works for him, to give the names of colours to his exhibition rooms of old masters. And the visitor to discover 'the pink room of the Bellinis, while the green, with its influences of Giorgione and Lorenzo Lotto was dedicated to Veronese, the red to Titian and to Tintoretto; there was even a grey room for the Canalettos, Bellottos and the Guardis.' As far back as 1548, in his *Dialogo di pittura* published in Venice, Paolo Pino had suggested a peaceful reconciliation between the merits of Tuscan *disegno* and Venetian *colorito*. But here it was merely a literary intention that had not the slightest effect on the art of his contemporaries, because the Venetians had, once and for all, abandoned draughtsmanship in favour of the magnificent primacy of colour.

One essay to the next gives the same naturalistic explanation for the supremacy of colour in Venice. 'It is not excessive, therefore, and concedes little to meteorology, to say that the secret of Venetian painting can be found hanging everywhere in the very air of Venice, in the light of that sky, multiplied in mirrors and veiled by the mists of those waters' Diego Valeri commented in *Guido sentimentale di Venezia*. It is as if the Venetian palette found its primary source in 'Venice's luminosity, in the inexhaustible chromatic variations of the Lagoon (with its nuances that vary with the depth of the sea bottom, all veined with currents, and marbled with marine prairies of seaweed, that change with the time of day and the flow that feeds it and the ebb that drains it, but always the gentle, wavering mirror of all the colours and all the tints of the sky, in its waters and muddy deeps' (Henri de Régnier, *L'Altana ou la vie vénitienne*). Painting and its colours reflect the Lagoon just as the Lagoon itself reflects the sky... 'Was it precisely,' Hippolyte Taine wondered after a superb description of the Lagoon, 'from a similar spectacle seen every day, was it from Nature whom they unwillingly accepted as mistress, was it from the imagination filled inevitably by the undulating, voluptuous appearances of things, that the Venetians' *colorito* came?' (*Voyage en Italie*). And what if the exact opposite were true? Without wanting to deny the fabulous beauties of the Lagoon, that on certain days can make us believe in the return of the gods, we must also recognise that even more often the Lagoon is flat, sinister, hostile, and it is undoubtedly in this way that it is perceived most frequently by the Venetians, who have never thought of their implantation in these miry swamps as a stroke of ecological good luck, or a picnic.

But nor must one think that this marvellous efflorescence of colour delights every visitor to La Serenissima. There are those who flatly condemn it, for example, the very puritanical Lucien Fabre, who would not rest until he could excommunicate the unpardonable crime against intelligence and self-awareness that repugnant Venetian sensuality represents, in which 'the four elements of nature make love; nothing can separate them and, in the richest among them, water, the four ruling elements melt in turn. Water varies at the sky's whim; it is a vassal of the winds; it panders to the moods of the earth, which it usurps as it flatters its reflections; it is in the image of the sun's flames whose spectra it fills with a million colours. The heavens are saturated with the vapour from its waters and human structures live there, tremble and move about like ships. I am not talking of the great medley of colours, nor of the mould, nor of the salty crusts with which the Lagoon, the air and the sun have ravaged the walls.' All this is only superficial sparkle, mistaken appearances, simplicity and deceit. 'In the simplistic enchantment of Venice I see a surfeit of organic satisfaction. The eyes engage in debauchery there' (*Bassesse de Venise – The lowness of Venice*). An inhuman plot against the abstract, the mind, ideas: 'Self-dissipation is perhaps the term that best reflects the dissolving effect of Venice's spectacular sights. A slow, conscious evaporation, in itself delightful, a disintegration into impalpable and even volatile elements, a dissemination of human life's participation in the universe in forms that are the most flattering to the senses. Visually, it is the variable infinity of colour juxtaposed to colour, in overlapping brushstrokes that pass unhesitatingly from one to the other through this seamless diversity, this iridescence of gross matter, wrack, seaweeds, this universe that is depthless, like a film of oil, a trap for lights where the light of the sky is fired with excitement or split ad infinitum, and achieves the perfection of continuity through the perfection of discontinuity. Precisely because we know that this can be explained (a question of retina, rods, cells, vibrations: another very intoxicating sort of poetry), we understand its seductive powers better: if this enchantment of vision is unique, it is because, through it, the best-made delight for our organs is offered to view, the physiologically exact answer to the problem of their desires' (*Ibid.*). La Serenissima is the 'country of the passionate palette' (Arsène Houssaye), so reprehensible and unforgivable a chromatic debauchery. Venice is 'an enemy of the mind', a prostitute-town ready to sleep with every colour. To be honest, if Venice is primarily playing a game with the senses, it just makes me love Venice more than ever.

And as if we had not had enough already of the sinister moralists of colour, Venice would become a refuge for all the Romantic Depressives on the planet. See Venice and die, in decadent mode. It has reached a point where no fewer than sixty tourists a year commit suicide in La Serenissima. And all the methods are good, from throwing oneself from a balcony on to the paving stones of a *calle* to a planned and calculated overdose in a luxurious room at the Danieli. It is quite possible though that many of those visitors who plunge recklessly into the nauseous canal waters to drown themselves, do not know that more often than not they can touch bottom and will generally emerge with just a sprained or broken ankle. Judging by the statistics (which were gathered with much seriousness by Dr Ramacciotti, a Venetian psychiatrist), it is the depressed, intellectual German homosexual who comes out top, Thomas Mann's model in fact, shortly followed by the love-lorn Anglo-Saxon, modelled on Shelley and Byron.

This can only happen as a result of not wanting to understand anything, or see anything in Venice, of simply choosing it as a romantic setting in which to commit suicide. Venice has nothing sinister about it, since all its aesthetic efforts throughout history have been precisely to fight against everything in its milieu that could possibly give rise to melancholy. My Venice, a city that the Venetians themselves have desired it to be, have willed it to be and created – not somewhere they have simply endured for survival's sake – is joyful and full of colour. 'The basis of the nation's character is gaiety,' Goldoni wrote, and 'the basis of the Venetian language is the joke.' There is no reason why in Venice colour is not part of the party, part of the celebrations. And in my celebration of Venice, colour by colour, I shall begin with the whites, which we shall rapidly pass over and forget, in order to reach those polychromes that are part and parcel of La Serenissima's true nature. I end my book with purple, an overloaded, almost congestive colour.

ೞ Limestone white ೞ

Think of all those imposing façades of palazzi and churches in white Istrian limestone. 'These rocks,' Francesco Sansovino wrote in 1581, 'that have been brought all the way from Rovigno and Brioni on the Dalmatian coast, are a sight to behold: they are white and similar to marble, but are hard and strong, and will resist the cold and sun for a long time.' Such whiteness, however, has never truly appealed to the Venetians, who will move heaven and earth to dispel and restrict the monotonous whiteness of the stone, and to give the façades of the palazzi, houses and churches colour. First are all the numerous incrustations of marble, those beautiful disks of porphyry and serpentine, that transform Santa Maria dei Miracoli and the Ca'Dario, as well as many other Venetian buildings, into precious polychrome shrines. Then there are all those frescoes that decorate so many of the palazzi. 'Giorgione', we are told, 'had painted some frescoes on the façade of his house at San Silvestro, and was summoned to the Grand Canal to decorate the Fondaco Tedeschi's façade, the most important of all the foreign commercial and financial centres, and Titian, who must have been eighteen at that time, also joined in this work. Following close behind, the Master of Castelfranco painted the façade of the Saronzo palazzo at Campo San Polo, then he was asked to decorate the façades of the palazzo Pisani and palazzo Gritti, on the Canalazzo at Santa Maria Zobenigo. Unfortunately all these works have been lost, as have the frescoes of Pordenone, which graced the front of the palazzo Morosini at San Geremia (demolished at the beginning of the last century), as have those of the palazzo

9

first called Anna, then Viaro, then Martinengo and now Volpi di Misurata. Lost too are the marvellous paintings of the great sixteenth-century masters that adorned the Grand Canal: by Tintoretto at the palazzo Gussoni at San Felice, by Veronese at the palazzi Coccina and Foscarini at San Stae, as well as at the palazzo Cappello at San Polo where frescoes by his rival Zelotti could also be found; those of Schiavone at Ca' Zane, Tiepolo at San Toma, Salviati at the palazzo Loredan at San Vio, Sante Zago at the palazzo Mocenigo at San Manuele' (Alvise Zorzi, *Il Canale Grande*). There are a few rare remains of frescoes by Camillo Ballini that have been preserved on the façade of the palazzo Barbarigo. Once upon a time the canals of Venice must once have looked like outdoor art galleries, an immense pinacoteca under the open sky. When the owners could not afford top-rank artists, who had achieved fame as painters, artisans were given the task of decorating the façades with ornamental patterns of leaves, vine branches, festoons, etc. So, although it is still colourful, Venice has lost much of its vibrant chromatic splendours, that have been remorselessly eaten away by chemical gases from the refineries at Marghera. La Serenissima must have been infinitely more sparkling in the sixteenth, seventeenth and eighteenth centuries. Yet, in spite of this regrettable discolouration and erosion, Venice remains as it always has been: an immense painted canvas. Very often one has the impression that this town exists only in and through its façades, that it is all on the surface, without any real depth, without a third dimension. It was already a *veduta* even before the painters of *vedute* became fashionable in the eighteenth century. As though it were just pure decoration painted on a surface, just walls bordering the streets and canals. Interestingly, the Venetians, who would sacrifice all for the sake of a showy façade, displayed extreme abstinence as far as the other walls of their dwellings were concerned. All the magnificent marbles and architectural inventions are reserved for the side which has its doorways opening on to the water. Only the visible part of the palazzo, in general, giving on to the canal where the gondola is moored, is well kept and valued. On the other sides are simple walls of brick without the slightest aesthetic refinement. When well away from the canals, in a narrow *calle*, you walk beside these very high, neglected walls, devoid of any embellishment, you can barely imagine that behind them there is a sumptuous *piano nobile* that opens on to the magnificent Gothic arcades of an elaborate façade.

❧ Graveyard white ❧

If you want the right atmosphere for a visit to the island of the dead, you must choose a particularly grey and sinister winter's day, when a cold damp fog blurs the contours of the palazzi and churches. You must first go to the Fondamenta Nuove, preferably first passing in front of San Zanipolo and the façade of the Scuola Grande di San Marco, which houses the Ospedale, and then walk along the picturesque rio de Mendicanti. You then have to pass in front of the great sombre vault of the boat garage, from where on some bad days ambulance boats and funeral boats depart and return in an incessant *chasse-croisé*, your walk then takes you in front of the San Lazzaro dei Mendicanti church which is part of the hospital and used only for funerals. And if you want to feel totally miserable, spend some time going round the cloister, which has been ruined by the different services the hospital dispenses. You will come upon the Lagoon, quite suddenly, shrouded in fog, where the huge orange balls of lampposts set on *dame* which mark the shipping lanes render the landscape even more lugubrious. After you have warmed up by drinking a few *ombre* in a café (or even one or several grappa, which may well be necessary) and after dawdling in front of two or three florists and funeral masons displaying their plaques and crowns, take the vaporetto No 5 to the island of San Michele, home to Venice's cemetery behind its huge pink walls all fringed with white and topped by the sombre green candles of cypress trees. You will pass the elegant, totally white, Renaissance façade of the church built by Mauro Codussi, enter the monastery, then cross the two cloisters, the first very old and very austere, whose four wings are paved with countess gravestones, and with an old well in the centre, the second more recent and jollier, with trees and flowers, almost a garden. You will begin to walk towards the old section of the *Evangelici* reserved for Protestants: here there is widespread decay, an unreal chaos in what is a sort of meadow planted with laurel, cypress, pines and palm trees, and cluttered with old monuments that, more often than not, are falling to bits and tumbling down. The cemetery itself is dying: there are broken paving stones, chipped and cracked plaques, overturned stelae, crosses falling apart and eyeless broken busts, their heads, eaten away and disfigured, have rolled aside from atop their bodies. Here all the usual funeral bric-à-brac is on show: tombstones, urns, truncated columns, marble crowns, weeping statues full of pathos, boastful obelisks, little angels and putti, busts, crosses, a marble anchor for a lieutenant commander. With difficulty I deciphered some inscriptions that were a little less worn than the others:

Eugen SCHUYLER
Statesman, diplomatist
Traveller, geographer, historian, essayist
at
the time of his death
Diplomatic agent and Consul general
of the
United States of America
in
Egypt
Son of
George Washington Schuyler
and of
Matilda Schribner his Wife
Born
Ithaca (NY), Feb 26, 1840

Died
July 16, 1890

Sacred
to the memory
of
William DRINKWATER
Born in Chepstown, England
17th January 1829
Died in the city
2nd August 1872
aged 43 years
Commander
of the
Cunard Steam-Ship
TARIFA
A beloved and devoted husband
A kind and affectionate father
Gone to be ever with his lord
Gone to receive his great reward
His end was peace

The Anglo-Saxons, narcissistic chatterboxes, can never resist recounting the whole of their life on their tombstone inscriptions, as if they were writing visiting cards or curricula vitae. I also noticed the relatively recent grave of John McAndrew, a specialist on Renaissance Venice, with this inscription:

O Venezia Benedetta
Non te voglio piu lasar.
[Oh, blessed Venice, I never want to leave you]

It is as though all the nationalities the world over made a rendez-vous with death in Venice. The tomb of a French knight, Guillaume de Freygang, graves of old American women, doubtless very old and very rich, and of young Englishwomen, who, at the age of thirty, came here to die of anaemia beside the Lagoon, of German baronesses and countesses, among them a certain Louise Taube, Russian and Polish princesses, including Anna Bagration and a C. Troubetzkoy (in the *reparto Greci*, the Orthodox section just nearby), consuls from every country in the world, from Norway, Switzerland, Sweden, the United States. The twin tombs of Sarah McLean Drake and her daughter Janet Drake, who died when a steamer sank beside the Lido on 19 March 1914. In the centre of a small lawn is Ezra Pound's grave, a simple oval bed of grass and flowers. At the head of the parterre is a low group of shrubs and a beautiful laurel bush at the foot of which is a stone, smothered in ivy, which simply reads: EZRA POUND. I have to say I dislike all this ostentatious vegetal simplicity that seems boastfully to defy Venice's minerality. A false sobriety. I far prefer the remorseless tumbling down of the old stones to the all too predictable triumph of nature. (When I visited the cemetery of San Michele again in July 1997, I must admit that Ezra Pound's grave had been completely redone, on the occasion of the burial of his companion Olga Rudge. Still fairly ridiculous, though, with its little border of stone and its frail begonias. The old laurel had not withstood the new arrangements: it had died. Perhaps such a remake was necessary to save the grave, in the midst of the immense devastation of the *reparto Evangelici*. For I found – I don't know if this is a purely personal impression – that the old cemetery was particularly ravaged and distressed-looking. As if a violent earthquake had felled and savagely broken all that had still been standing. In less than two years, this *reparto* had aged enormously. Could it be a consequence of the extension works of San Michele, just next to it? Or quite simply that these old corpses had had their time. New graves chasing out the old, almost all irremediably crumbling and illegible: now Asians are replacing the Anglo-Saxons.)

Only after this can you wander through the gigantic modern cemetery, with its many new quarters. This is a completely different town, one similar to Venice, its double, with its rich quarters and its poor quarters, its luxurious individual residences and its high-rise housing in dovecote form, with specialised zones for the military and for children, its pariahs thrown into a communal trench or hounded out of their individual graves and relegated to ossuaries. A completely industrial and prisonlike urbanisation of death. Quite a few people have devoted page upon page of moving and depressing writing to San Michele, for such a place seems to them to call for it, where death itself, cynically commercialised and managed, re-enters the economic cycle of consumer goods. As far as the eye can see there are immense fields of uniformly white crosses, with an infinity of vases filled with flowers, mostly artificial and vividly coloured, to the point where the visitor might sometimes be tempted to wonder if it is 'a cemetery or a delirious planting by a horticulturalist who might have mixed floral species and colours' (Brice Matthieussent, *San Michele*). Yet, despite this wintry weather, and the fogs that discolour the Lagoon, San Michele has nothing truly sinister about it: it is too big, too demonstrative, too spectacular, too exhibitionistic.

Nor am I ignoring all the heartbroken and dutiful writing inspired by these countless photos fixed to the white crosses that turn the cemetery into a nostalgic family album or an out-of-date police poster, whatever you choose. 'San Michele, the island of the dead, is a vast gallery of hidden portraits. Some of those who have passed on seem to have posed looking their objective straight in the eye, smiling and trusting, as though standing beside a painted liner or a coconut tree on a canvas background in the photographer's studio. Others appear to have been taken by surprise: that man there, with his head in his hands, bent over a book, seems to be saying to death that it has disturbed his reading.

He would much rather wait, at least until the end of the chapter' (Edwige Lambert, *Arrêt sur image – Pausing on the Image*). Nor can I ignore all the melancholy, even depressing feelings that these faces can inspire, faces that are about to fade away irrevocably, many already blurred and worn away, eaten by rust, attacked and pitted by salinity, wrinkled and blackened by damp. Sadness, despondency, time's wingèd chariot that absolutely refuses to 'suspend its flight', etc. And yet San Michele, this castle of death solidly anchored in the Lagoon (and that is the most important point), does not arouse in me that desperate feeling of dereliction which seems appropriate to these places, if one is to believe the majority of foreign visitors. And, what is more, the Venetians love strolling here as a family on a Sunday, with no particular feelings of sadness. Undoubtledly they see San Michele, with its architectural monumentality, as one more challenge to the laws of nature. The Venetians would only be devastated by their cemetery if one day, as has happened at fort Sant' Andrea, a large chunk of the brick walls, undermined and excavated by water, were suddenly to detach itself from the encircling wall, and the dead themselves topple over the edge and flow body and goods into the Lagoon. Dying, after all, is casting anchor and it is out of the question that the great vessel of stone, afloat on the waves, or rather on land, the cherished remains of parents and friends, should sink in the vile muddy swamp of the Lagoon. 'I hate San Michele cemetery,' one of the characters in Pier Maria Pasinetti's *Rosso veneziano (Venetian Red)* recognised, in spite of his family's reassurances. 'It frightens me. It's sinking. It's going down. All Venice is sinking into the water, everyone knows it: a little bit each year... I wake up at night and I see our dear departed under water in the mud of the Lagoon; I see them all engulfed...'

☙ Moonlight white ☙

A never-ending *leitmotif* of all the literature devoted to La Serenissima is that the moon purifies Venice, turns her white, redeems her, saves her momentarily from her remorseless decline. While in full daylight the city shamelessly exhibits her lamentable old age, her abundant mutilations and incurable infirmities, night rejuvenates her, gives her back all her youth, all her splendour of yesteryear: 'Venice, seen at night, seduced and enchanted me: that moonlight, those shimmering stars, that calm scented with poetry, that limpid and quivering earth gave her an indefinable attraction, and some fairylike quality.

'Daylight came and disillusioned me. On the dirty, unsavoury water floated and drifted cabbage and lettuce leaves, bits of straw and old corks. The houses, horribly damaged by an unfortunate dampness, made it all too aware that sections of their walls had "endured waves and the painful outrage of the years"' (Camille Villeneuve, *Deux mois en Italie – Two Months in Italy*). For a few hours the moon heals and hides those wounds and suppurations, the moon re-enchants Venice, reactivates her attractions, neatly outlining the contours of palazzi and churches, leaving the frightful leprous rotting of bricks and marble in the shadows: 'I would that I could evoke the moonlights, but it is impossible. Venice by moonlight is an enchanted city: the floods of silver light upon the moresco architecture, the perfect absence of all harsh sounds of carts and carriages, the never-ceasing music on the waters produced an effect on the mind that cannot be experienced, I am sure, in any other city in the world'

18

(Benjamin Disraeli, *Letters*). As in a M.G. Lewis gothic novel, it is a return of the Romantic, of political and amorous intrigues, in the old city deserted so long ago by her doges and her courtesans. Once again, La Serenissima finds her ardour and her passions of yesteryear, acts and conspires: '. . . under the mellow moonlight the Venice of poetry and romance stood revealed. Right from the water's edge rose long lines of stately palaces of marble; gondolas were gliding swiftly hither and thither and disappearing suddenly through unsuspected gates and alleys; ponderous stone bridges threw their shadows athwart the glittering waves. There was life and motion everywhere, and yet everywhere there was a hush, a stealthy sort of stillness, that was suggestive of secret enterprises of bravoes and lovers; and clad half in moonbeams and half in mysterious shadows, the grim old mansions of the Republic seemed to have an expression about them of having an eye out for just such enterprises as these at the same moment. Music came floating over the waters – Venice was complete . . . In the glare of the day there is little poetry about Venice, but under the charitable moon her stained palaces are white again, their battered sculptures are hidden in shadows, and the old city seems crowned once more with the grandeur that was hers five hundred years ago . . . once more is she the princeliest among the nations of the earth' (Mark Twain, *The Innocents Abroad*). In moonlight the peaceful Serenissima, great consoler of our woes, once more regains calm and silence that put our anxieties to sleep and pacify our passions: 'When the wind at midnight passes over the lime trees and shakes the flowers on the water; when the perfume of the geraniums and clove trees ascends in gusts, as if under the moon's gaze the earth exhales embalmed breaths of air; when the cupolas of Santa Maria raise into the heavens their hemispheres of alabaster and their minarets crowned with a turban; when all is white, water, sky, marble, Venice's three elements, and from high up in the tower of St Mark's a great bronze voice floats over my head, I begin to live only through my pores, and bad luck to whoever might call upon my soul. I vegetate, I rest, I forget' (George Sand, *Lettre d'un voyageur*). Much good may it have done dear Aurore Dupin, baronne Dudevant. May she rest in peace then after her tempestuous, torrid affairs with Alfred de Musset and Pietro Pagello, and may she celebrate with so many writers and painters (especially Whistler) the ethereal glamours of nocturnal Venice. I shall let them get on with it, but will not share their enthusiasm. For, to be honest, I am not really seduced by this rather glaucous, milky Venice, which is much too clean and too white, saved from herself, superaestheticised by this lunar unreality which in the eyes of so many visitors makes of her a marvellous 'legendary décor', the brilliant silver furrows of the boats, trembling reflections of lanterns on the canals and water glistening in the velvety blue night. As it is, the wearing effect of all the poetic sentimentality about moonlight is considerable and exasperating, especially when Venice needs daylight to be truly herself, to exist fully. For Venice exists, it has nothing of a vague misty dream, of an impalpable poetic dreaminess. It is not ethereal. It is very real. It is the 'soft and soporific Venice' invented by biased languid somnolent foreigners that is unreal, and that disappears as soon as they return to their homes with the first chill at the end of autumn: 'One fine morning,' Rainer Maria Rilke wrote, 'the other Venice will be there, the real living Venice, as fragile as glass and which has nothing of a dream about it: this Venice born in the middle of a void, built on submerged forests, this product of will, conquered by force and become at last real from one end to the other. A toughened body, reduced to the barest of essentials, across which the Arsenale, active day and night, speeds the blood of its labour and the spirit of this body, a penetrating essence which never ceases to spread, stronger than the perfume from the lands of spices. And the skilful State, which exchanged the salt and glass of its poverty for national treasures. The beautiful city which acts as a counterweight to the world, full of latent energies present even in its ornament, in its ever finer ramifications – that is Venice' (*The Diaries of Malte Laurids Brigge*).

Venice is to be taken *en bloc*, such as it is, uneven and heterogeneous, with its beauties and its wounds. Rather than the empty lyricism of lunar white, I shall always prefer the more trivial white of sheets, tablecloths and household linen, impeccably washed and ironed that, very early in the morning, the overladen barges carry from the laundries to deliver to the restaurants and hotels of the still sleeping town.

The tragic white of
⌇ Pulchinella ⌇

It is obvious right away that the crowd is cruelly mocking a clown as he performs his acrobatic tricks and piles buffoonery on buffoonery. Dressed in a wide floating tunic in different shades of white, he has a tall, stiffly starched, pointed hat which is also completely white. He is congenitally misshapen and awkward, hunchbacked, pot-bellied and has a big bottom. His caricature mask is in the grotesque, changing colours of the Cucurbitaceae, which earns him the name of *cetrulo* – cucumber. He has the facial features of a cock with his long hook nose (defined in ancient times as a *pullus gallinaceus*). He usually speaks in a falsetto voice. He has little talent as an acrobat, and is a crestfallen good-for-nothing charlatan. He is always ridiculous, but even his ridiculousness is vaguely disturbing. You have surely recognised Pulchinella, a famous character of the original Commedia dell' arte of the Campania, the Neapolitan masker *par excellence*, whom Giandomenico Tiepolo adopted and acclimatised to Venice. On the walls of Villa Zianigo di Mirano, near Mestre, that the son of the great Giambattista covered with frescoes just after the fall of the Republic in 1797, he frolics in every possible situation. On the ground floor is a whole world of Pulchinellas simultaneously grotesque and pathetic: Pulchinellas on a swing; mounting a donkey; Pulchinellas enjoying themselves as they watch performing dogs; Pulchinella walking in the rain; chasing a young peasant girl; holding his son in his arms and watching two other Pulchinellas walking on their hands; Pulchinella in love; Pulchinellas relaxing in the shade of a pine tree after a game of racquets. It is in vain that they pretend to play and enjoy themselves, for they experience no true joy. More pitiful than festive in their excessive, caricaturish attitudes, and always deformed in these frescoes, the colours of which are undeniably cold. They play all life's roles. Sufficient to say that at this extreme end of the eighteenth century, there were only Pulchinellas left in Venice, only empty masks. From all the evidence Pulchinella fascinated Giandomenico, since he made a long suite of 104 drawings chronicling the life, adventures, death and miracles of Pulchinella, entitled *Amusements for children*. For children, we may well ask? For, if a certain number of drawings seem to reveal a comic innocence, many others, in contrast, have nothing funny about them, and are closer to Goya's nightmares than the usual innocent facetiousness of the Commedia dell' arte. When a platoon of Pulchinellas fires on three other Pulchinella prisoners, for example, or when a Pulchinella is hanged in front of a sober assembly of other Pulchinellas. When the skeleton of a Pulchinella, recognisable from his hat, appears on a grave in front of other Pulchinellas who are running away, terrified. It is no coincidence that Giandomenico Tiepolo chose this Neapolitan character to incarnate the anguish of a Venice that had become politically outmoded, dispossessed of itself: its choice of painter is at least as chromatic as it is psychological. Visibly, white disturbs Venice, undoubtedly because white, although the sum of all the colours in the spectrum, is perceived as an absence of colour. Zero degree of colour, to say the least, causes anxiety for a people who are so warmly chromophile. Interestingly the Venetians had a name – *larva* – for the white mask that always accompanied the classic *bauta*, the Venetian disguise *par excellence* that comprised 'a black silk cape and a short cape or rachet of black silk, which began at the head – on which was worn a black tricorn hat – and came down to the shoulders, thus covering half the body.' To this was added a false face almost always white, the *larva*, which both men and women used indiscriminately. In Latin, *larva* means a spectral figure, the *larva*, the phantom and even the mask of the phantom, and in fact ' in moonlight, in a town lit only by the light from the *codegas*, Venetians coming home from a night of pleasure at the theatre, brothel or gaming table at the house of some patrician, must certainly have looked like mournful ghosts with these white "faces" surrounded by so much black' (Danilo Reato). They had the unnerving appearance of bats, all these nobles such as seen in Guardi or Longhi's paintings of the *Ridotto*, the gambling house that Marco Dandolo had opened in 1638 in his palazzo of San Moise. White also is the plague doctor's mask, the grim reaper of Venice, with his spectacles and very long curved beak full of aromatic essences, medicaments and disinfectants. Such a dreadful bird of ill omen, with his long black oilcloth cape.

∽ Tintoretto's white ∽

While it is true that we tend to censure the modern fashion for pictorial detail that is so rife at the moment in many art books, providing us with expensive, luxurious albums of photographic enlargements of figures and landscape that might well have escaped our attention in the course of our aesthetic contemplation, the fact remains that this macroscopy, though overdone and monstrous in many cases, sometimes gives us unexpected insights and surprising revelations. Take, for instance, Tintoretto's immense *Crucifixion*, painted in the Sala dell' Albergo, on the first floor of the Scuola Grande di San Rocco. Right in the background, at the very back, we can see insignificant, tiny figures who make up part of the crowd present at the death of the Son of God. Human creatures rapidly and summarily sketched in a few nervous strokes, in a few white lines, are lightly highlighted with touches of oranges and reds. There are two ordinary little men walking along together, of whom one, an anguished old man with coal-black eyes and a long beard, is leaning painfully on a crutch. Another is crossing a sort of bridge, carrying a stick on his shoulder. These are barely human figures that are strangely disturbing, *larvae* who have just emerged out of nothing and are condemned soon to return there, I couldn't say exactly. Graphically the same can be said for *The Baptism of Christ* which is also in the Sala Grande of the Scuola: in the background are distant silhouettes of the crowd assembled on the riverbank, their white features visibly drawn at great speed. If then you go to the Galleria dell' Accademia and if you look at *The Theft of the Body of St Mark* by that same Tintoretto

25

(who moreover was originally a member of the Scuola Grande di San Rocco), you can't help noticing the strange décor of the scene. That false Alexandria, in fact the Venice of the Procuraties, is like alabaster, almost ethereal when the weather is really bad. While right in the foreground a group of people, of Christians of Alexandria, of a prodigious muscular and plastic vigour, violently projected to the fore, are carrying away the remains of the saint in order to save his corpse which is about to be burnt on a bonfire, that great heap of faggots visible on the canvas, the whole background is occupied by figures and discoloured architecture, whitened, pallid, almost translucid. Everything unfolds in a dramatic and oppressive atmosphere. A low, stormy sky, leaden, almost black, with white zigzags of lightning: the storm is about to break. The infidels are escaping, some on foot or on horseback, under the arcades of a building that remind us of those in the Piazza of St Mark's, undoubtedly more terrified by the miracle than wanting to escape the torrents of water that are about to beat down. Spectral, phantomlike and Islamic constructions. A ghostly and deadly whiteness. With all these strange whitened threads spread just about everywhere, some of which seem to sketch the figure of an angel. In truth, Jacopo Robusti, known as Tintoretto, the little dyer, is also an astonishing bleacher. If Tintoretto is a prodigious colourist, it is no less true to say that the use of colour barely wins over an ever possible return of the curse of white.

∽ Blue water ∽

Sky blue, as others would say? But it is not so obvious in Venice where the narrow labyrinth of *calli* generally only allows you to see tiny patches of sky. There are hardly any escapes to the sky, unless you are going down the Grand Canal or walking along the quays that run alongside the Lagoon. The blue here is primarily the blue of water when it is – rarely – in good health: 'This moving blue water is a good sign. It indicates that the Lagoon is living, oxygenated and habitable: with the slightest variations of depth and temperature, it changes colour and "thickness" on a scale never seen. In fact, if we go out into the open sea we can see here, if we look closely, that the water is made up of minuscule suspensions: as if the hand of God, this night, had spread ashes there. In the great shallow stretches it is still pale: it would need another storm for the blue to spread as it should, but there are already blue, almost black, circles, all around. Were the sea to be narrow, perhaps it would turn openly into a small summer green (Paolo Barbaro, *Lunazione veneziane – Venetian Lunations*). So be it . . . the blue of the Lagoon water when it is on form. But to be honest I have never found many convincing blues in Venice. Apart, perhaps, and very contradictorily, the gentle serene blues of the pleated garments of Giovanni Bellini's sweet Madonnas and the disturbing blues of the police boats' flashing lights.

∞ Venetian blonde ∞

'Burn a faggot of vine twigs, riddle the ash, put it in a small canvas bag. After that, have the cleanest earthenware vessel you have, at the bottom of which you place the barley straw, and over the straw, three drachms of myrtle leaves, three of boxwood sawdust, and the same quantities of saffron, cumin and cypress flowers. You must put the cumin in a bag which is wide enough to cover the whole vessel; and over everything, and before it boils, throw in the ashes of the vine twigs described above; wash your head well; instead of soap, use alum and rub it in with great care. But you must not clean your head the next day, the concoction must have time to take effect. Wash your hair, leave it to dry by itself. The following morning, by some means, make the water left in the retort come out quite clear and bathe your head in it, for in this water thus prepared I recognise a virtue such that I believe it will render your hair similar to the colour of gold.'
This is one of twenty-six recipes, each and every one more minutely described and more complicated, offered to the Venetians by a doctor who originally came from Modena, Giovanni Marinello, high priest of blonde hair, who, in 1562, published a treatise on women's finery, *Gli Ornamenti delle Donne*, as well as a book devoted specifically to the art of hairdressing: *Nel quale si dimostrano le naturali belleze de capelli e li artificiali come acquistar si possano (In which are shown the natural beauties of hair and how to procure some artificial hair if you can)*.
Would you like another recipe which is just as Borgia-like in its extraordinary mixtures? 'You will have hair like gold if

you take 3 drachms of rock alum, 3 of turpentine, one of saffron, 4 of madder and 2 of vine ash. Pound the madder with the ash finely, boil it in water until the water has reduced by a half. Sieve the residue, and mix in the alum, the turpentine and the saffron. Keep this true ornament of your grace in a large phial. Then when you would like to make yourself blonde, you first paint yourself with it carefully and minutely and bathe your hair with a sponge soaked in this mixture: as soon as your hair is dry, wash it in water in which clover, barley, cumin and soap have been boiled. I believe it is unnecessary to praise this remedy to you since you can imagine its value for yourself.'

The other great specialist in transforming brunettes into blondes is the knight Leonardo Fiovaranti, who in 1675 published *Il Compendio de' Secreti razionali intorno alla medicina, chirurgia et alchimia* (*The Compendium of Rational Secrets of Medicine, Surgery and Alchemy*). Here is one recipe from the great many the book contains: 'In Venice, they make a sort of blond water which is truly very fine, and which makes blond hair very light, a shade very much in favour with the patricians of that country. One takes washing-water in which dyers have boiled silk, and for each pound one adds one ounce of ash of tartar, and washes one's hair with it and stays in the sun until it is dry. And as I have said to you, the hair attains a shade of blond which is almost white, or to be more exact, ashen. Once the hair is dry, you rinse it in a vapour of yellow sulphur; you will then have a more pronounced blond colour. Such is the mixture that most of the Venetian ladies use to make themselves blonde.'

A final recipe is even more astonishing: 'Place a good quantity of sunflower seeds in the milk of a woman who is suckling a male child and leave them for ten days. Pound them all together and squeeze out the oil in a press. The properties of this oil are extraordinary for, if you anoint your hair with it, it will look like the finest gold; and if you bathe your face in it and rub it in well, it will become perfectly clean and so beautiful it will seem divine' (Giovanni Dolcetti). If so many recipes exist which differ so much one from another, then in fact there were numerous shades of Venetian blond, with a scale that ran from the most brazen, to the gentlest pink, to crude bright red, to ashen and the finest moonlight shades.

It must be added that in reality all these preparations, all these mixtures were still not enough to obtain the fashionable Venetians' most sought-after type of blond, which involved exposing their hair to the sun for long periods. 'Ordinarily,' wrote Cesare Vecellio in his *Degli habite et moderni di diversi parti del mondo (On clothes and Fashion in Diverse Parts of the World),* published in Venice in 1590, 'the roofs of the houses in Venice are crowned with small wooden buildings which take the form of belvederes open to the day. On terra firma, this type of loggia is made of masonry and is tiled like those that are called *terrazzo* in Florence and Naples, and are covered with cement, sand and lime to keep out the rain. It is here that Venetian women frequently spend their time, far more than they spend in their rooms; it is here that, with their heads exposed to the heat of the sun, for whole days at a time, they strive to augment their charms, as if they needed it, as if the assiduous employment of so many procedures known to all did not expose their natural beauty to the risk of being referred to as artificial. At the time when the sun throws its most vertical and baking hot (*cocente*) rays, they climb on to these little wooden loggia and condemn themselves to be grilled and served up there themselves. Seated, they bathe and rebathe their hair relentlessly with a sponge soaked in the waters of youth prepared by hand or bought. No sooner has the sun dried their hair than they quickly bathe it again in the same mixture, once more to be dried by the fire from heaven and once again carrying out the same procedure. This is how they make their hair blond as we see it on them. When they sacrifice their time to this activity, they cover their garments with a very white silk dressing-gown which is very fine and light, and which they call a *schiavonetto*. They also cover their head with a hat that has no crown, and through the opening they pass their hair which they spread out on the brim so that it is exposed to the sun throughout the whole operation.' I love to imagine those sixteenth-century Venetian women installed on their perches, high up in their palazzi, wearing their *Solana*, that hat that serves both to dry their hair and as a parasol to protect the neck and their pale skin, from the heat of the sun's rays. A white, female forest of living chimneys alongside the traditional Venetian flared-cylinder chimneys, the upended cones that can be seen in great numbers in the paintings of Vittore Carpaccio and Gentile Bellini. After this, all they had to do was carefully comb and curl this artificially blond hair, often making curls which began at the ears and went straight up as far as the highest part of the forehead. This means that the famous Venetian blonde had nothing natural about her, it was a fashion which was all the rage in the sixteenth century, and so one can better explain the extreme deception of the Abbé de Bernis, French Ambassador to Venice in the seventeenth century, desperately searching here, there and everywhere, in the *campi* and the *calli*, for true Venetian blondes, who if natural were pretty rare. He encountered only magnificent heads of ebony hair, for the great fashion of the Venetian blonde had passed. It was the end of those splendid flaming yellow heads of hair with long golden tresses.

∽ Brocades ∽

1949. Orson Welles was about to embark upon the costly and interminable shooting of *Othello* in which he himself would play the role of the Moor of Venice. While he was looking for some sumptuous and luxurious costumes worthy of his *mise en scène*, he made a visit to Mariano Fortuny, by then retired, and cloistered in his palazzo Pesaro degli Orfei, set back from the Grand Canal, on the corner of the modest and silent campo San Benedetto. At first things went badly between the enthusiastic and larger-than-life filmmaker and the famous couturier, now tired and old – he would die just a few months later. Happily, the everflowing loquaciousness of Orson Welles, who grew more and more impassioned as he explained his researches for Othello's costume, succeeded in drawing Fortuny out of his lethargic melancholy. He disappeared into a room, and came back with an armful of costumes, from which he drew out a jacket in grey-green brocade, lined throughout with grey fur, spotted with white. Welles tried it on in front of a mirror, and contemplated the figure that looked as though it had stepped out of a painting by Carpaccio: the costume was exactly what he was looking for. The fur especially looked completely Renaissance. When he asked where it came from, Fortuny suddenly sprang to life. It came from some Australian moles, he said, moles which fed off the corpses of their own kind: cannibal moles. And suddenly, full of joy, he declared that it was a brilliant way to breed for it solved the problem of feeding without involving any expense. What a brutal and cruel rejoicing. The ferocious

32

underside of the magnificent spectacle, the barbarous lining to the brocade. In fact one could not imagine an outfit more suited to the tragic destiny of Othello, killed by jealousy. Desdemona was this cannibal fur. And it was, equally, highly appropriate for Venice, where the most sumptuous brocades hid the most pitiful settlings of accounts against anyone who, rightly or wrongly, was suspected of threatening the Republic's institutions: doge, patrician or a just an ordinary citizen, ruthlessly eliminated by burning, poisoning or drowning. Totally indifferent to his times, to its innovations, to its aesthetic modernity, Mariano Fortuny shut himself away and dreamed of resurrecting the ancient splendours of Venice, of a Renaissance finally rediscovered through the medium of the most splendid and richest fabrics. It is a true to say of Venice that its colours and fabrics are inseparable, its colouring is based on textiles.

The technique of velvet, of Chinese origin, was most probably introduced into Italy via Persian weavers exiled in La Serenissima, which very rapidly became the centre for silk-weaving. Its artisans produced velvet studded with gold, reminiscent of the splendours of Saint Mark's mosaics, playing on the contrast of gold with a muted colour – reds or greens. One of the most original of Venetian creations was cut velvet. 'This technique consisted of shaving away the tops of the fine loops of silk [to create what is known in English as tufted pile]. Then, by cutting the strands into two, sometimes three, different heights (using the technique known as *altobasso*) it became possible to create patterns in a magnificent relief. [This is known in English as pile on pile velvet.] The matt and brilliance of the weave create changing refractions of light in the red, violet and turquoise-blue tones of the silk. But the velvet most admired was still the 'ironwork' or 'antique' velvet [known in English as ciselé velvet]. This was a unicolour velvet of emerald green or ruby red, into the pile of which patterns were hollowed out or chased (ciselé), imitating the openwork form of ironwork or stone mullions in the windows of Gothic churches. The contrast between the light tone of the satin and the deep tone of the cut velvet achieved an effect of relief never seen before, through the range of different depths obtained' (Jacques Anquetil). Consequently colouring amounted to clothing, the hues were those of textiles.

'Venetian painting,' as Mary McCarthy pointed out in *Venice Observed*, 'from beginning to end is a riot of dress goods.' On a more technical level as well, Venetian colouring was inextricably linked to cloth. For with the Venetians 'the background was not limited to a middle colour in the scale of colours. It involved the texture of the canvas. The operations of *il colorito alla veneziana* depend upon and exploit the interaction of woven fabric and medium, from the effects of the dry brush leaving a veil of broken colour in its wake, to the determined opacity of thick impasto, imposing its own heavy substance upon the canvas. Between these poles of visual and tactile experience lies the record of the painting's progress, as well as its mimetic referent' (David Rosand, *The Meaning of the Mark*).

You could say that reconstituting and reviving the sumptuous old fabrics of Venice in keeping with the style of the times is also an exercise in discovering the architecture of the city. It is no coincidence that Marcel Proust re-found the entire Serenissima in the superb Fortuny dress that his companion wore: it ' seemed like the tempting shade of that invisible Venice. Like Venice, it was smothered in Arabian patterns, like the palazzi of Venice, hidden in the manner of the sultans, behind an openwork stone screen, like the bindings in the Biblioteca Ambrosiana, like the columns whose oriental birds alternately signify life and death; these ornamentations were repeated in the shimmering of the fabric, which was of a deep blue and which, as my gaze advanced upon it, changed to melting gold, through those same transmutations which, before the advancing gondola, change the azure blue of the Grand Canal into blazing metal' (Marcel Proust, *La Prisonnière*). And we have all been tempted at one time or another to see in La Serenissima's buildings incredible displays of sumptuous, skilfully openworked textiles and fabrics. 'Just as lace is a fabric in itself and not an embroidery on a background support, the architecture of Venice is a mirror open to the sky and light. It is not the spaces here that define the façades, but the windows. The walls are openwork, just as lace is made with see-through stitches. The background, no less than the design, owes everything to the working of the extravagant decoration. Neither the ornament nor the daylight add anything to the framework: they are the framework. And just as the design of lace has limits unknown to embroidery, Venetian architecture is limited in every sense by the expanse and level of moving water in which the architect places his foundations and his floors' (Andre Suarès, *Voyage du Condottiere*). Even the most modest buildings have 'a suppleness of cloth, gently following the contours of the routes of earth and water' (Liliana Magrini, *Carnet vénitien – Venetian Notebook*). The old marbled floors of Saint Mark's have the gentle undulations of oriental carpets. And especially, when they have just been washed by rain, the marble facings on the side of Saint Mark's 'look like oiled silk' (Mary McCarthy, *Venice Observed*). All the marbled surfaces of Venice are like satin. Even the ducal palace does not escape this vivid textile structure, 'a suspended mass festooned with the warlike lace of its crenellations and striated with the rose coloured arabesques that are seen in basketwork' (Henri de Régnier, *L'Altana ou La Vie vénetienne*). And even in denigrating Venice, Herbert Spencer, who detested the pattern covering the walls of the Doge's Palace, because in his opinion it looked more like a piece of knitting than masonry (and he may well have had a point here), recognised the influence of textiles on Venice's architecture. The list of similarities continues still further, as when, for instance Henri de Régnier went to the island of San Lazaro: 'From far off the brick walls of the old convent looked like an ancient brocade, coloured pink, from which stood out the sombre velvet of the cypresses. One could say it looked like the motif on some oriental fabric or the design on a Persian carpet.' Even its setting by the sea does not escape the spreading infection of textiles. On some winter days traces of mud transform 'the water into an infinitely soft and ever-changing silk' (Diego Valeri, *Fantasia veneziana*), in a Venice that weaves a delicate cocoon of peaceful splendour around itself. There are other moments where the Lagoon becomes 'a fluid and subtle cloth that a flock of gulls embroiders with a fleeting arabesque' (Henri de Régnier, *Ibid.*). If I have such a fondness for the precarious, flimsy Venices drawn by Théo Tobiasse, it is because of their delicate unravelling of indecisive, quivering lines, that remind me irresistibly of those small doilies my mother used to crochet. Like a lacemaker's design, his style of drawing seems to run along and wind itself into a ball, like a fragile, magic thread.

If there is one walk that I ritually make every time I go back to Venice, it is the one where, once I have walked the length of the Fondamenta Nuova, if I then turn to the left, takes me towards the Campo dei Gesuiti. A small tranquil square that is ravishingly provincial, with its well, as in every *campo* in Venice. But there is a surprise. The modest houses, which carry the names of the old streets reminding us of the ancient guilds of *sartori* (tailors), *tessitori* (wool weavers) and *botteri* (coopers) are dominated by a marvellous church. Santa Maria Assunta dei Gesuiti, built 1715–29, to plans by Domenico Rossi, has a splendid exuberance. From the start the grandiose, Baroque façade designed by G.B. Fattoretto is very promising in the very way it thrusts upwards, with eight high Corinthian columns supporting a narrower second storey, and in perfect balance, very high up on the tympan, and etched against the sky, the contorted statues of the Holy Virgin of the Assumption being carried off into heaven by the angels, of course. And, in addition to all this, inside the building, there is the enormous pleasure that, every time, is just as fresh and unspoilt, of rediscovering an incredible mineral brocade, a complex marquetry of ancient green and white marble that covers all the walls with leafy branches and flowers. What a joy it is to walk on the elegant marble paving, and to feel underfoot that carpet of green and yellow marble that covers the steps to the main altar. One can hardly dare imagine the cost of the colossal amount of work that was expended, the most skilled artisans in Venice covered the whole nave with incrustations of marble. The whole interior of the building has been decked in magnificent brocades. For this was the decorator's real intention: to dress all the walls with a sumptuous marble cloth, to give to this church, simultaneously, 'the intimate grace of a bedroom and the pomp of the opera' (Henri de Régnier). The main altar, with its eight cabled columns in antique green looks more like a four-poster than a sacred place. The pulpit especially, outstrips all expectations, looking like the rich tent of a Renaissance prince, with its draperies, its lambrequin, its pompons. All those innumerable complex marble pleats. And on each new visit, I cannot resist going up to the main altar, as naively as the first time, to verify what the carpet is made of – marble, obviously.

On great feast days, the Venetians love to deck the columns in their churches with heavy red brocades, for they can only imagine their architecture splendidly dressed.

Flesh colour

Would I have enjoyed fucking a Venetian courtesan? Or might I, instead, like the very wise (too wise) Montaigne, have been content to read an interminable elegy composed by Veronica Franco, no. 204, out of 215 inventories in the *Catalogue of Venice's Most Famous and Most Honoured Courtesans*. Average price asked by a lady: two crowns, which was not really the most expensive at that time. 'At best Montaigne would have come out of it with the pox,' Paul Morand noted maliciously. And he was probably right: I have very serious doubts about the pleasures afforded the author of *Essays* by the literary quality of this Venetian lady-of-the-night's outpourings, although as one of the most frequently sampled courtesans, she became famous as a poetess. But, by then, she had retired from business. Or might I perhaps have hankered to be with Agatina, bedecked with jewels like a nymph, on her bed in her small beautifully furnished palazzo, 'the most splendid of all the Venetian courtesans' if we can believe Charles de Brosses? 'Truly,' he added, 'she is the least pretty of all the first rank; but on the other hand, who can deny that the favours of a hand smothered in diamonds are not truly precious?' Might I have fallen for the attractions of La Padoana, the Paduan, who made it a point of honour to pay in kind for the ducat that Jean-Jacques Rousseau left her? Poor Jean-Jacques emerged more disturbed than gratified or thrilled by this gallantry, convinced that he had been seriously pickled by the encounter and was ripe for a spell in the Hospital for Incurables. If it is true that two creatures by Carpaccio in the

Museo Correr are actually courtesans, as is suggested by the title of the painting given it by Ludwig and Molmenti,* I have grave doubts that I would have any desire to obtain or rather purchase the favours of these two impassive, sourfaced, somewhat disturbing women, 'with a chignon atop their head and frizzled curls on either side of their face'.

If, on the other hand, I were able to obtain the favours of certain other Venetian women whom other Renaissance artists have painted, then most certainly I would not have hesitated for an instant. How could I not have wanted, even for a single night and at no matter what price, to share the bed of these pretty women? How could I have resisted the charms of those beautiful, firm but opulent breasts that are entirely exposed to view in Palma Vecchio's *The Courtesan* (Museo Poldi Pezzoli, Milan), *Flora* by Paris Bordone (Musée du Louvre) or *Woman Revealing her Breast* by Tintoretto (Prado, Madrid) who is undoubtedly someone other than Veronica Franco, or indeed Parrasio Micheli's *Courtesan with a Lute* (Szépmüvészeti Museum, Budapest). All those naked breasts peeking out from ample white blouses! And, more importantly, how would I not have tried to obtain by any means possible the favours of Giorgione's *Laura* (Kunsthistorisches Museum, Vienna)? How

---

* We know that the panel in the Museo Correr in Venice, depicting *Two Venetian Women*, and that in the J. Paul Getty Museum in Malibu, depicting *Hunting Ducks on the Lagoon*, in fact make up the two separate parts of a unique ensemble forming the continuous decoration of a small door within a larger one. 'These are, therefore, two noble and virtuous women who, according to the escutcheon on the vase of lilies, may have belonged to the Preli family, if it were not for the fact that this house died out some time in the twelfth century. These honourable ladies are with their husbands who are enjoying the pleasure of the chase, be it real or metaphorical. The beat on the lagoon is evoked through an enchanting vision which, having the characteristics of the countryside, thus effectively establishes a unity of place and time between the world of reality and that of imagination. In order, so it seems, to ensure the connection between these two entities and their mutual involvement, a child placed on the ledge of the parapet is moving forward to enter the physical space occupied by the two women' (Vittorio Sgarbi). The title of *Waiting* is given to this geographically separated ensemble. All that is left to say is that the two wives are treated more by way of satire than compassion.

could I not succumb to the enigmatic charms of her slightly round, plump face and her pretty naked breast which nests snugly against the fur? A tender nipple sensually nestling: for the woman is naked under her garment. One knows, after reading Cesare Vecellio who is an authority on Venetian costume (*Habiti antichi et moderni,* 1590), that one typical type of dress worn by courtesans in La Serenissima during winter was precisely a jacket lined with a warm, sumptuous fur ('*vestida da carno, con veste foderata di bellissime pelli di grand valore*'). For this not so slender and so little idealised Laura is of course a courtesan, despite the branches of laurel framing her face and resonances of Petrarch's Laura and of the challenge he made in his two sonnets on Simone Martini's portrait of Laura: how can one transcribe such perfect beauty into a pictorial image? In fact the name of Giorgione's Laura is only a pseudonym, a 'nom de guerre' since it was the custom for these hospitable women to adopt a famous name from history or literature.

According to critical tradition Giorgione was the true inventor of female flesh in Venice. 'In colours he found an impasto that made such mellow brushstrokes that never existed before him: and it must be said that these brushstrokes are just like flesh infused with blood, and executed with so much ease that it is no longer a matter of pictorial illusion but rather of truth to Nature; for in the shading of the colours (that can also be found in Nature), in the highlights and the halftones, in the touches of reddish colours, whether weak or strong, he achieves such an agreeable and authentic harmony that we must call it painted Nature or painting imbued with Nature' (Marco Boschini, *Le ricche minere della pittura veneziana – The rich sources of Venetian painting*). Giorgione 'acquired a sense of colour, managing to reproduce to perfection the freshness of living flesh . . . the strength and the roundness with which Giorgione skilfully endows his figures does not, as with other painters, prevent his colours from having beauty and his flesh tones a great sanguine, almost flamboyant audacity' (Anton Maria Zanetti, *Della pittura*

Veneziana). The same can be said for Titian, who learned much from Giorgione, and whose female flesh has warm and soft colours. If this painting gives the onlooker so much satisfaction, it is because its material effects, inflexions of the pressure of the brush, impasto, direction and swiftness of the strokes lead, as David Rosand has already shown, to a truly tactile expectancy, a quite tangible presence of the mimetic. 'In the processes of Titian's *colorito,* substantiality is correlative to proximity; the very build-up of paint brings the rendered object that much closer to the viewer, who is invited (*pace* Vasari) not to stand back and squint until a focused illusion is obtained, but rather to approach to respond to the tactile appeal of articulated stroke and surface' (*The Maker and the Mark*). The desirable body surges from the chromatic substance itself. If, in the final stages of a picture, as Marco Boschini reports, Titian painted with his fingers as well as with the brush, it was because he had to remain, tactilely, in contact with the body. The poet Paul Valéry was not mistaken when he said: 'One has a great sense that, with Titian, when he gently arranged a Venus of the purest flesh on a crimson drape, in the fullness of her perfection of a goddess and of a painted thing, *painting* was caressing, joining two voluptuous activities into one sublime act, where the possession of oneself and one's methods, the possession of the beautiful woman are in every sense blended together' (*Degas, danse, dessin*).

Always we have this appetising golden blondness of female flesh, at least when it is painted, for in reality the Venetian woman, as men desired her, is '*bionda, bianca* and *grassotta* – blond, fair and plump.' It was very important for Venetian courtesans to keep their skin and complexion fair. 'They liked', as Tomaso Garzoni records disapprovingly in the sixteenth century, ' to make themselves beautiful with different unguents and cosmetics, emptying the shelves of grocer's shops of white lead, chloride of mercury, alum mixed with plaster or with egg white, crystal flower, refined borax; they gave themselves sparkle with the soft part of bread, distilled vinegar, broad bean juice, and with the liquid from bullocks' droppings like the cows they are. They freshen their faces and soften their flesh tones with almond water from Persia and lemon juice; they try to preserve their beauty with roses, wine, alum . . . '

Is Venice nowadays still the city of illicit love? All the hoteliers in La Serenissima will always swear that as far as legitimate couples go, there are the newly weds on their honeymoon, with gondolas and serenades, the lot, or tender, decrepit old couples, celebrating their silver or golden wedding – but these do not make up the greater part of the visitors, far from it. Happily otherwise. I recall the frightening image of a couple of newly weds wandering through the Giardinetti and the piazzetti, he in his official black suit, she in a long white dress, with her little bouquet in her hand, visibly lost and disorientated, while many tourists, delighted to find a living postcard at hand, rushed to photograph them. For a moment I could not help wondering if they had been paid by the tourist board. In fact, from all the evidence, they were not Venetians, and may be they had travelled (by train, car, plane?) in their wedding attire, or perhaps they had changed into it in their hotel room in Venice. There was nothing more painful, more indecent than the way they felt obliged to show that they were happy by kissing in public. Even thicker on the ground, and a cause for rejoicing, are the illicit couples stealing a few days' happiness away from their solitude or from the daily greyness of their marriage, or those who come to Venice in search of an encounter. That fifty-year-old woman, on her amorous jaunt to Venice with her young lover, was most probably right when she 'imagined all the couples naked in bed' in this ancient gallant city. 'It was quite obvious that when they travelled to this town a man and woman made love at least once. So all the couples one met must have just fornicated, something one could not imagine happening in any other place in the world, something stealing through the air, like an additional entertainment' (Michèle Manceaux, *Pourquoi pas Venise*).

⟣ Local colour ⟢

Every aesthete nowadays, who despises the common tourist, firmly believes that, in Venice, you must at all costs avoid St Mark's Square and its immediate surroundings, the Procuraties, the Merceria, the Riva degli Schiavoni, as well as the Rialto, all of which are invaded by swarming hordes of tourists, barbarians and ignorant people, along with their fatal companions, the souvenir salesmen. Authentic Venice lies elsewhere, in the Canareggio, the lively working-class *sestiere* of artisans and shopkeepers, in Castello with its shipyard workers and fishermen, in Dorsoduro where students and artists, writers and painters take refuge. And it is true that nowadays the Venetians, driven out by exorbitant rents, have been pushed further and further towards the outskirts of Venice, or even Mestre, the worst of all possible exiles for them. The true Venice of the Venetians is essentially on the outskirts. One morning, as you cross the Dorsoduro, begin taking a walk, very early on, towards the rio San Trovaso. On the way, take time to admire one of the oldest types of workshop (*squeri*) where they build and repair gondolas. Don't delude yourself too much though! This workshop is, unfortunately, now no more than a picturesque, part-time activity – essentially no more than a postcard. Now continue your itinerary by following the quay, the Zattere al Ponte Lungo, in the direction of the port. You pass in front of the headquarters of the great maritime companies, in particular, the Adriatico (for marine insurance), in front of the harbour master's office, the maritime health services, the maritime veterinary services, maritime radio. You will discover a completely different Venice, the town port bustling with activity, which does not survive solely on tourism. A real, living Venice that is not reduced to a melancholy memory of its former glory. The people you pass are in their great majority of pure Venetian stock, sailors, workmen, office workers, housewives. Behind you, far away, the great monuments are blurred in a haze of heat. In the background are tankers, cargo boats and great white steamers at anchor. Nothing is better suited to the old established, flamboyant marble buildings at the water's edge than their high, proud metallic structures and brilliant colours. How modern Venice is in never refusing other worlds, either geographical or temporal. On the other side of the canal is the Giudecca, with its factory chimneys and great claw-like cranes. Walk as far as the Stazione Marittima which, if you are merely a visitor, you cannot enter. Then linger at a table on the terrace of the Trattoria Borghi, just in front of the San Basilico vaporetto stop. The owner won't mind if you don't want to eat – not even a murmur – since he knows that you just want to sit down, wait, look at the fleeting colours, savour the atmosphere, take your time. The true Venetian knows full well that history has come to a standstill in his noble city, and one has all the time in the world to take one's time, and one must make use of this pause to do nothing. But if you ask him for a glass or two of white wine, take an *ombra* the way Venetians do, you will give him enormous pleasure, he will hurry to serve the wine very cold, engage you in conversation, exchange the trivia that forms the basis of any socialising between strangers. Here, essentially, are only true Venetians, and they still take pleasure in welcoming us because we are the visitors, the minority, because we are not a part of the invading hordes. So take your time, take an interest in the incredible traffic on the canal which opens its wide mouth on to the Lagoon: there are police and military speedboats, transporters with their bent beaks carrying vehicles from the Tronchetto to the Lido, the profusion of potbellied barges loaded down with crates of vegetables, cases of drinks, furniture on the move, building materials. Here the utilitarian reigns supreme over the aesthetic, or rather the utilitarian, while submitting to the exigencies of navigation, itself becomes aesthetic. Transported on the water, the most trivial of objects acquires a strange, sometimes almost surrealist beauty. Vaporetti offload their cargoes of chattering Venetian women, each one trailing a still empty shopping trolley. It is simply that in Venice you yourself have to transport all your purchases, and constantly assess their weight, their awkwardness. It is impossible to go shopping by car to some hypermarket or other, a reason for not encumbering yourself with provisions, you do not stock up in advance. You live from day to day. Now you can take the vaporetto, the 82, to Sacca Fiesola.

You are now on the other side of the canal on the Fondamenta Beato Giuliano. Poor public housing, with masses of multi-coloured washing, vests and pants for the whole of a week, hanging from the windows, a few trees, a few shabby, yellowing patches of grass for children's games, a football pitch. This is the end of the harmonious colour combinations of historic Venice. Huge lazy cats overwhelmed by the heat. On the bank there are fishermen's hoop nets with wooden pickets to moor them in the Lagoon. You come to a *cantiere navale*, AMAV Venezia, where modest barges lie face down on bare grass. There are factories that are more or less abandoned, military land overgrown with brambles, canals muddy and bogged down, whose banks are littered with masses of blackened debris. Here the border between water and land becomes more and more uncertain. Venice is basically nothing more than this moving and troubling uncertainty. Each time you find it, you are truly in Venice. And it is difficult to fight the sensation that at any moment this island could suddenly detach itself from the town and be lost, sunk for ever in the Lagoon. Strictly speaking, Venice is not sinking into the mire, rather the movement of water caused by the huge numbers of motor boats is destabilising and shaking the larch piles on which the whole city is built.

Time to continue the walk by crossing the wooden bridge over the Canale dei Lauraneri that leads to the main part of the Giudecca. You will come upon an immense disused factory, a gigantic neogothic fortress of triumphant capitalism, with battlements and little towers, that is undergoing rehabilitation: this is the back of Mulino Stucky. Continue beside the canal past other abandoned factories, past the Women's prison, a disturbing and moving building, and further on you will find several secret properties that must have been very desirable in their era of splendour, and if you should happen to take the route I took, you will discover a beautiful garden with an entrance gate that has two delightful decaying *putti* on either side: their broken legs leaning against the rusting ironwork. They are fragmented, falling to bits, eaten away, disfigured, but nevertheless remind us that, even in these places that look the most destitute in Venice, no one has relinquished the appeal of love and licentiousness. When you return to the bank, you come to the church of San Eufemia, inside which is a superb holy knight by Bartolemeo Vivarini, as always in a glorious bright red. Now that you have found the official splendours of Venetian painting and colour once again, you are conscious that you have already returned to the borders of that other Venice, which is no longer truly the city of present-day Venetians.

So must one, for all that, consider that this Venice, so often in very bad taste in its summer get-up, the Venice of foreigners and tourists, is totally false and artificial? People who reproach La Serenissima for the barbarous medley of colours of her cosmopolitanism remind me of those devotees of painting who feel that there are too many pilgrims at Assisi to allow for a proper, leisurely study of the frescoes of Cimabue, Giotto and Simone Martini. Crowds of foreigners have been part and parcel of the Lagoon city since time immemorial. 'Venice responds to its eternal genie by welcoming the joyful, multi-coloured flood of foreigners on holiday... crowds that in no way mar a city permanently devoted to carnivals, travel and exchange. They form an integral part of an unforgettable spectacle, as the two small red marble lions beside the basilica can vouch with their deeply worn backs used by fifty generations of children from all four corners of the globe to leapfrog. They are the children's mischievous version of St Peter's feet, worn by a thousand years of pilgrims' kisses' (Michel Tournier, Les Météores). Look at the swarming cosmopolitan, European and Oriental crowds in the paintings of Gentile Bellini and Vittore Carpaccio. And, are we right to level our criticisms at the unfortunate Japanese when we denounce the horrors of the development of tourism, if we remember that one of the most famous Venetians is none other than Marco Polo, son of rich Venetian merchants? He left Venice with his father and uncle in 1271, reached Peking in 1275, worked at the court of Kubla Khan, founder of the Yuan dynasty in China, before finally returning to Venice in 1295, after twenty-five very long years abroad. It was Venice which went in search of Asia first. From time immemorial, Venice has welcomed and loved its many-coloured crowds of every nationality: 'The flood of crowds is as indispensable to the façade of St Mark's as the water of the canals is to those of the palazzi. While so many ancient monuments are misused by the tourist who simply dashes into them, and appear to us as though they are being profaned, even by us of course, when we do not go there with the intention of serious study, those reserved, secret, closed, forbidden places, rudely ripped open, those places of silence and of contemplation brusquely given over to chatter, the basilica itself, along with the town that surrounds it, has nothing to fear from this crowd, and from our own frivolity; Venice was born and has continued under constant public gaze from visitors, its artists have worked in the midst of the conversations of sailors and merchants. Since the beginning of the thirteenth century, this façade has been a shop window, a display of antiquities. In reality, what has prolonged Venice's life are the shops under the arcades' (Michel Butor, *Description de San Marco*).

∞ The colours of music ∞

'It is like a ray of sunshine bursting into the gloom or shadows,' the *Harmonie universelle* (published in Paris in 1636) tells us. I really like this solar luminous, almost pictorial and chromatic definition of the dazzling sonority of the cornett, the baroque trumpet *par excellence*, that instrument of awakening, of the very Resurrection itself, which resounded so magnificently in Claudio Monteverdi's *Mass of Thanksgiving* sung at St Mark's on 21 November 1631. In one sense the Basilica's *maestro di capella* was only repaying his debt. The plague, that had cruelly decimated La Serenissima, had in fact been brought from Mantua to Venice in the course of the summer of 1630 by a diplomatic mission that had at its head Alessandro Striggio, a lifelong friend of Monteverdi and the librettist of *Orfeo*. More than 80,000 Venetians perished during that terrifying epidemic. Towards the end of the summer of 1631, the plague began to lose its virulence and finally disappeared during the autumn. The authorities decided to celebrate on 21 November with a day of rejoicing and of the most sumptuous magnificence, on the occasion of the feast of the Presentation of the Virgin Mary at the Temple. Hugh Keyte has described how the Doge and the Signoria descended in great pomp towards the piazza San Marco, black with people, where a notable representing the Ministry of Health announced the deliverance of the city. Twelve trumpets and twelve snare drums sounded a fanfare, some *codette* (small, very vociferous cannons) were fired, and the bells of all the churches rang out. The *Mass of Thanksgiving* that followed was one of the most grandiose of the whole of the seventeenth century. The Madonna Nicopeia

– the miraculous icon of Our Lady of Victory – a Byzantine image which came from Constantinople and which is still in the left transept of the basilica, was displayed on the main altar, surrounded by a great quantity of lights. The Minister of Health made a triumphal entrance with trumpets and drums, which, contrary to custom, remained inside the church afterwards. When one reads records of the period, what impressed Monteverdi's contemporaries most was that he had combined the trumpets with voices in the *Gloria* and the *Credo*.

Very few among those who have listened to Vivaldi's *Four Seasons* concertos may know that the music is rigidly descriptive and follows a fixed programme laid down in four sonnets that were perhaps written by the Red Priest himself. Here the music forms a picture, imitating not only the sounds (during spring: bird song, streams ruffled by breezes, thunder and lightning, a dog barking to the moon; during summer, the songs of the goldfinch and the turtle dove, the gentle summer breezes and the wind from the north, the buzzing of flies and midges), but also depicting atmospheres, scenes of daily peasant life in Venetia. Take winter, for example:

'Shivering and frozen amidst the cold snows
Under the cruel breath of a horrible wind,
Running and the stamp of feet at every moment
And also the chattering of teeth,

'Passing near the fire and peaceful gentle times
While outside the rain soaks more than a few
Stepping gingerly and slowly on the ice
Moving prudently for fear of falling.
'Going fast, stumbling, falling down
Setting off again on the ice and running fast
Until the ice splits and breaks,

'Feeling the Sirocco pass under closed doors,
Boreas and all the winds at war
Such is winter, but what joy it brings!'

At first, as H.C. Robbins Landon points out, the 'string orchestra enters, a part at a time, beginning with the bass, to tell us of a frozen landscape in the Veneto, the human "frozen and trembling" (the latter = trills in the violins). Later, in a fierce section...our legs are shaking with the cold; and ...there are double stops in the solo violin to imitate chattering teeth. The second movement, a Largo, describes sitting in front of the fire, while the rain (violins pizzicato) beats outside, in contented E flat. Anyone who has experienced the driving rain in the Veneto will remember the delight of escaping into a room with a roaring open fire, spits of game turning slowly in front of it. In the next movement, Allegro about walking on thin ice...the solo violin slithers about in quavers, with no supporting harmony whatever; and after two pages of score, we slide carefully in slurred quavers – walking very carefully so as not to slip. But we try just the same to walk quickly and do slip, falling...we try again, with staccato semiquavers. The ice breaks...The south wind blows outside the tightly fastened doors in another beautiful Lento, which with hesitant pauses, leads to a violent series of passages in the solo violin; the north wind arrives and gives battle to all the other winds' (Vivaldi). From this one can see that the aim of this music is to make images, to convert the sound into pictures. To say of music that it is highly coloured has undoubtedly become the worst of stereotypes: nevertheless in the case of Venetian music this expression expresses the literal truth.

Even if it is just a legend (which quite probably goes back to Marco Boschini's book, *Le ricche minere della pittura veneziana*, published in 1674), I still like to believe that the four musicians who feature in the centre of Veronese's *Marriage at Cana* (Musée du Louvre, Paris) are indeed painters. The artist in a white smock in the foreground who plays the viola da gamba would be a self-portrait of Veronese himself. The other musician in the foreground on the other side of the table who is all dressed in red would be Titian in person. Behind, in blue, is Tintoretto, holding a small violin, and finally Bassano, wearing a felt hat, blowing into a straight cornett. After all, if one is to believe Vasari himself, Veronese first became known for a painting with a musical subject: *Music* (Venice, Biblioteca Marciana). 'The painting which earned him victory and this mark of honour is an allegory of Music in which three ravishing young women figure: the most beautiful is playing a violin da gamba, her eyes lowered on the neck of the instrument and her ear cocked in the attitude of someone listening attentively; of the two others, one is playing a lute and the other singing in accompaniment. Nearby a wingless Cupid plays the harpsichord, showing that music is born of love, or rather that love is always a companion to music and, so that love never leaves, Paolino has shown him without wings. In the same painting he has painted Pan, the god of shepherds according to the poets, holding those bark flutes that some victorious shepherds in the music competition have offered him by way of an ex-voto' (*Lives of the Painters*). And were not Venetian painters very often excellent instrumentalists? Giorgione, who gave musical instruments such importance in his frieze at Castelfranco, loved playing the lute and sang so divinely that people of quality summoned him for their concerts and parties. Was not Sebastiano del Piombo a musician before he became a painter, as was also Paris Bordone who was primarily an excellent lutenist? Jacopo Tintoretto played several instruments, and Titian had, in exchange for a portrait, ordered a portable organ from the famous manufacturer Alessandro Trasuntino. If so many Venetian painters cultivated this art, it is not only because the perfect courtesan had also to be an accomplished musician, but because Venetian music, particularly when it had to be adapted to brilliant ceremonial in the basilica of St Mark's, was always spectacular. It entered the realm of vision. Venetian music is a pleasure to the eye.

✑ The colours of painting ✑

In the month of May 1544, Pietro de Aretino had just, unusually for him, eaten alone, or rather in the unpleasant, tedious company of ague which made it impossible for him to enjoy any food. To change his frame of mind and stave off boredom, he leaned out of his window and watched the Grand Canal: 'the marvellous spectacle of countless boats, full of passengers from here, there and everywhere' and the entertainment on offer from two boatmen who started to race each other. He took 'pleasure in watching the crowd which had gathered on the Rialto bridge to see the race, and on the Camerlonghi quay, as far as the Pescaria, the *traghetto* of Santa Sofia and of the Casa da Mosto.' Finally he looked up at the sky, 'which never since God had created it, was adorned by such a delicious pictorial play of light and shadows. The air was of the sort that those [painters] would like to express who envy you because they cannot be you.

'First the houses, which though made of solid stone, seemed to be of an unreal substance. And then imagine the atmosphere, in some parts limpid and fresh, in others murky and sombre. Judge my amazement at the sight of those great clouds, masses of dense vapours, partly low and heavy on the roofs of the houses and partly in the middle distance, so that on the right everything was misted over in a greyish black. I stood admiring the diversity of the colours playing on these clouds: the nearest burned like the flames of a fire from the sun; the more distant ones all reddened with the less intense heat of red lead. Oh with such beautiful strokes did Nature's brushes sweep back the atmosphere, clearing it

53

far away from the palazzi, just as Vecellio [Titian] has done in his landscapes. In some places a bluish green appeared, towards others a greenish blue, tones truly composed by a caprice of Nature, the mistress of masters. With the help of lights and darks, she gave the effects of depth or relief to what she wanted to advance or retreat; and I, who know your brush as the very soul of her spirits, exclaimed to myself three or four times: "Oh Titian, where are you now?"' Yes, this whole description of a sunset on the Grand Canal features in a letter written to Messire Titian in person. In writing this, he was replying to Vasari's criticisms in his first edition of *Lives* in 1550, when he said that colour allows Titian to go hand in hand with Nature, which herself does nothing more than the painter. Exactly as his friend Lodovico Dolce would do in 1557 in *Aretin: Dialogue on Painting*: 'This is the marvel of it for in him alone (and let it be said without him becoming acrimonious with others), one sees combined to perfection everything that has been shared out elsewhere, for as far as *invenzione* goes, just as *disegno*, nothing will ever surpass him. As for colour, no one can rival him. Of such kind that to Titian one can give the palm of perfect colourist, something that no one among either the Ancients or the moderns merits, something that no one else can claim for themselves; in fact, as I said, he works like Nature in every way.' Aretino chose Venice as a perfect example of this specifically chromatic character of Nature, which behaves in just the same way as a painter. In Venice, being is pictorial. 'Here everything becomes and everything ends up as a painting...Because against this sky, these waters, this atmosphere, which secretly transmutes stone, brick and their geometries into pure colour, into pure pictorial values, there is really nothing more to it. Because, when all is said and done, it is from painting that the substance, the intimate essence of the city is made' (Diego Valeri, *Guida sentimentale di Venezia*).

∽ The colours of the seasons ∽

'They say that in each season,' Liliana Magrini remarked, 'the light extracts the colours that suit it from the town, as though from a multi-coloured palette.' On winter days, it is 'lemon yellow, acid, very tenuous: as if by some miracle extremely delicate nuances of this colour appear on the rough castings one thought were grey. I cannot explain how one finds it again, in a very pure form, on all the boats that have been given a new coat of varnish: usually it is red that has been used as a base' (*Carnet vénetien*). In fact a similar sudden winter appearance of the colour is rarely mentioned by writers on Venice, who almost always turn a moment of sinister discolouration in the town into the rainy season: 'After midday the fog descended, soft and heavy, in a few instants extinguishing all the colours, unravelling all the shapes: the buildings flowing together in vast masses of shadows, the water becomes opaque, dead, the bends of the canals filling up with grey cottonwool, the lamps veiled, each enclosed in its brief halo above the blackened and viscous paving stones. Black shadows spin away before lighted shop windows; one of them stops at the glowing brazier of a chestnut seller, then just as quickly disappears and vanishes in the void' (Diego Valeri, *Fantasia veneziana*). Then if it has just snowed, delighted photographers can have a field day, thinking they will be able to provide an image of Venice which is truer, more authentic because unexpected: the plain colours of the canvas coverings – the blues, reds or turquoise green are masked, a white mantle cloaks the black gondolas now at rest. From high up in the campanile, one can see that white roofs have replaced Venice's usual red. And on the campo San Bartolomeo, Goldoni who had seen it many times, watched the snow fall. But in Venice the snow remains decorative and almost festive. The needy lacemakers of Burano even have a stitch that is called snow. The patterns of the lace are raised, enriched with a multitude of tiny picots, themselves raised by other picots, the whole top-picoted: giving the lace an effect like snowflakes. In contrast, there are other moments of winter when the grisailles of water and sky meld, making you despair of the town. I remember once when I stayed over the Christmas holidays and my annual rediscovery of Venice had not brought me the immediate happiness that I had anticipated. Grey was the mirror of the Lagoon, grey the low ceiling of clouds that covered it, grey the palazzi and the churches blurred by a curtain of rain. Water oozed from everywhere. Near the Frari, I had eaten an abominable pizza which seemed to have gone soggy with damp, it was spongy and sticky. And when I had arrived at St Mark's Square, I could have sworn it was covered by the *acqua alta*. You could no longer distinguish the boundary between watery sky and water, or between canal and pavement, between Lagoon and drowned city. The water had drunk the horizon, absorbed the town that was saturated like a sponge. Everything was flowing together, disintegrating, dissolving. Raindrops dripped down my face, my clothes were wet, and I knew that it would be difficult drying them in my hotel room. The water, which welled up in the cracks between the paving stones and the bottoms of walls, soaked up any courage, any desire to be happy. So my joy was unimaginable when, at the end of the afternoon, I discovered the fair set up along the Riva degli Schiavoni. Immediately my good spirits returned when I saw the dazzling displays of the fairground stalls, the bunches of multi-coloured balloons. Neon lights lit up the fête. Strings of small flying saucers, with their winking lights rose and fell as they swung around, dodgems slid across their brilliant floor, the illuminated caterpillar charged along its rails. I could not be forgiven. I had doubted, I had lost confidence, when experience told me that one could always rely on the Venetians to dissipate gloom and fight melancholy. 'To amuse oneself in Venice is an institution; miserable people do not know how to amuse themselves' (Claude Michel Cluny, *Le jeune homme de Venise*). I had stupidly given way to spleen. Nothing is more out of place in Venice than being miserable.

If the winter is often considered as the *nec plus ultra* of Venetian authenticity, summer, in contrast, ought to be the height of artifice. Tourists arrive in hordes at a time when Venetians are hurrying to leave the stinking Lagoon for the healthy pleasures of the countryside on terra firma. And, as regards colour, the heat has effects which are as devastating as the winter fogs. Too much light dazzles and blinds, extinguishes the most sumptuous polychromatic effects. If one is to believe writers about Venice, the two real seasons of colour are spring and autumn, when the return of fine weather refreshes and revives La Serenissima's dying tints. In the month of April 'even the stones grow green again,' George Sand exclaimed ecstatically. 'Be in no doubt, my friend, what Venice is. She had not taken off the mourning clothes that she wore in winter, when you saw those old pillars of Greek marble, whose shape and colour you compared to dried bones. Now spring has breathed on all that like emerald dust. The foot of these palazzi where the oysters cling to the stagnant moss, is now covered with tender green moss, and gondolas slide between two carpets of this beautiful velvet green...All the balconies are covered with pots of flowers and the flowers of Venice, that have germinated in warm clay, open in moist air and have a freshness, a richness of fabric and a langorous pose that makes them like the women of this climate, whose beauty is as dazzling and ephemeral as theirs' (*Lettre d'un voyageur*).

When autumn finally arrives, writers about Venice feel nothing. The season before in fact symbolises the final glories of Venice at the end of her history. And here is

D'Annunzio, celebrating in his pathologically narcissistic and amphigoric prose, the still more magnificent evening hour when in autumn the genial poet, drunk with poetry and beauty in his gondola, had the impression of following 'the funeral procession of Summer, of the dead Season', that moment that he has also called Titian's moment, 'because everything finally glitters with a very rich gold like the naked figures of that prestigious workman and seems to illuminate the sky rather than receive light from it. From its own glaucous shadow there emerges the octagonal church that Baldassare Longhena borrowed from *The Dream of Polyphilus* with its cupola, its statues and balustrades, strange and sumptuous like a temple of Neptune which, one could say, imitates the torsions of seashells, the white of mother-of-pearl where the diffusion of salty moisture seems to create in the cracks of the stone a gemlike freshness which gives them the appearance of pearl valves half open in their native waters' (*Il fuoco – The Flame of Life*).

∞ The colours of feelings ∞

In Venice in 1525 Mario Equicola published his *Libro de natura de amore* which would start a flood of small treatises devoted to the relationship between love and colour...It could be that colours have certain characteristics that truly signify love, and all these treatises offered their readers 'secret messages to the loved person through the way one dresses, liveries or markings, insignia, or even through the offering of a bunch of flowers of different colours' (Manlio Brusatin, *Storia dei colori*). In 1528 it was the turn of Antonio Tiselio to publish, in Venice, again, which is the capital of colour, his *De coloribus*. Then in 1635, yet again in Venice, Fulvio Pellegrino Morato brought out *Il significato de' colori*. In his brief treatise Morato specified that 'the significance of colour will only have an "insignificant" objectivity if it does not conform to the *convenientia* and to the *adherentia*, contrary to the paradox of "*soi-disant* philosophers who will swear that snow is not white but black"'. A short piece of poetry (a sonnet) usually preceded these exercises in interpretation, each line translating the language of a colour as a resumé of the joys and sorrows of life, and especially of human behaviour: twelve colours were described, to which were added the heraldic colours of gold and silver. Here 'green represents hope; red, vengeance, cruelty, massacre; black, the pain of love and death; white, purity and truth, sincerity of heart; yellow, domination and arrogance; tan or fawn, fearlessness, royal grandeur and recognition for good deeds; ash and beige for cunning; crimson, the pleasures of love; a rainbow

59

of colours, bizarreness, fantasy, instability; turquoise blue, elevated thoughts; gold, riches and honours; silver, mistrust and jealousy; yellowy green, hopeless despair' (Manlio Brusatin). How far removed this language of Renaissance colours is from our present-day sensibilities. Why make lamp black or purple agree with leek green when we other modern people are inclined to consider that the purple and green pairing is one of the most vulgar and consternating there can be? Why consider that this same purple is an 'austere' colour, the opposite of *crisocolla,* malachite green, which represents florescence? The authors of those times themselves were well aware of the random and arbitrary nature of such a language of colours: when Fulvio Morato published his treatise, he entitled it, as though mocking himself, *Iris od operetta dedalea dedicate al Contrario* (The Rainbow, or Daedalian opuscule dedicated to Opposites). It just shows that symptomatically Venetians feel the need to place their psychological world of feelings inside a chromatic one. Here love itself is a question of colour.

⁓ Gilt ⁓

When you walk down some of Venice's meandering shopping
streets, in particular, in the area around the peaceful campo
San Barnaba where there are still many art craftsmen, and you
linger at the shop windows, you cannot help but notice,
almost immediately, the incredible number of objects that the
Venetians have gilded: mirror frames and picture frames, the
ornate wood of armchairs and of baroque-style couches,
angels in wood or resin, even masks, from the simplest
maschera to a face composed of sun and moon combined. And
there are also all those incrustations of gold on Murano
glassware for even glass must be gilded, integrating gold into
its airy transparency. To do this, the skilful artisan must apply
very fine pure gold leaf on to the surface of the incandescent
glass bowl. When the glassblower blows through his hollow
rod, the glob of glass expands and the dilation of its surface
turns the leaf into sparkling gold dust. Another famous
speciality of the Murano glassblowers is the *mosaico d'oro*.
Some very fine gold leaf, made by gold beaters, is glued with
egg white on to a very thin sheet of glass. The whole is then
put into the furnace and a second coat of melted glass is
poured on to the gold leaf. All that is left to do then is to cut
the whole into tiny tesserae.

Every surface that can possibly be gilded, every material
that can possibly be mounted or set, and even others, the
Venetians will, just for the sake of it, cover with brilliant
gilding, enrich with a few milligrams of precious metal.
Since time immemorial the gilder's complex art has been an
integral part of life in Venice. When one looks into public

records and private documents of Titian's period, one is overwhelmed. 'It is madness, folly: everything is a question of gold. The houses are in marble and gold. The interiors of almost all the aristocratic dwellings are decorated with gold and silver wall coverings, the steps of the stairs are embellished with gold, the beds are of gold, their clothes are in gold brocade. At the palazzo Vendramini, the columns are of oriental jasper, the doors encrusted with ivory and ebony. However, one day the Venetians noticed that something was missing. And immediately they began to gild the candles which gave them light, then the pâtés, the oystershells, the crabshells. And finally bread' (Ferdinand Bac, *Le Mystère vénitien*). The interiors and the furniture acquired it too; in the hall of the Palazzo Cornaro, the fireplace is decorated with gold caryatids. And if it was forbidden to Venetians to decorate the gondolas belonging to private houses, they made up for it by outrageously decorating the dignitaries' great gondolas, manned by four rowers, in particular those of the foreign ambassadors, the cabin of which was in gilded wood and hung with gold awnings. And of course the Bucintoro was no exception to the rule, decked out entirely, as it was, with statues, in particular a monumental effigy of Justice, and gilded haut- and bas-reliefs: rich décor in ciselé gold which served 'to show the people their princes in all their magnificence' (Goethe, *Italian Journey*), except in its seaworthiness, for this triumphal boat, which was badly proportioned because it was overloaded with ornamentation, had too shallow a draught and was scarcely able to cope with a puff of wind, let alone the high seas. And on Ascension Day, at the time of the Feast of the Marriage of the Sea, the most sumptuous of Venetian festivals, the doge, in full regalia, wearing his *corno d'oro*, a gold silk damask pallium, and boots sewn with gold thread, was himself a golden idol in this vain piece of theatre that the gilded barge was, like the Host in a monstrance. Then, at the porto di Lido, he would throw a large gold wedding ring into the water. I believe I read somewhere that a swimmer used to recover it. This is not dissimilar to the case of the rich Labia family, who had the spectacularly extravagant habit of throwing all their gold plate out of the windows of the palazzo, at the end of their splendid banquets, when, in fact, early the following day, they made sure the servants retrieved it pretty quickly in fishing nets specially laid on the bottom of the canal. Whether this is true or pure malicious talk we don't know. But, if it involved the Venetian nouveaux riches, it would not astonish me, for nouveaux riches are what the Venetians will always be.

This mania for gilding is characteristic of the parvenu who must put everything on display for all the visitors. So it comes as no surprise that the Venetians pulled out all the stops in the basilica of St Mark's, the 'chiesa d'oro', a nouveau riche confection, with its mosaics that are like 'so much basketwork in gold' (de Goncourts). 'I float in a dream of gold,' André Suarès wrote ecstatically. 'I am caught in a snare of gold, I rest on gold and I swim in gold. I have gold under my feet. I have gold over my head. Golden air touches and flatters me. And the incense is a golden vapour. The deep and distant windows filter gold, across a coloured glaze of yellow horn; and the gold insinuates itself, like a subtle wave, between the naves, bathing each pillar. And who would not be moved to walk on the rounded, billowing russet paving stones, clinging like turtles to the subterranean wave which carries them? The piles of St Mark's should be in gold, a forest of ingots planted in the Lagoon. A quadruple heart of gold, four wells of dreams under four cupolas' (Voyage du Condottiere). If I am honest, I have to say that I find nothing more repellent than the Pala d'Oro, the gold reredos which has been La Serenissima's pride and joy for centuries: of all Venetian works of art, it is without doubt the one I can stand least. A monstrously extravagant construction in gold smothered with more than 2,000 precious stones (526 pearls, 330 garnets, 320 emeralds, 255 sapphires, not counting the amethysts, rubies, agates, the topazes, the cornelians and the jaspers – and the 255 enamelled plaques and medallions. Here quantity far outweighs quality, even if the frame of the reredos is just a thick plank of wood covered in gold leaf: impress the gallery, but do not spend needlessly where it cannot be seen. Also gilded are the guardian angel high up in the campanile of St Mark's and the lion of the clock tower. Everything always has to be gilded, even the pierced frames of the windows and the caps of the mooring posts for the gondolas on the Grand Canal, even the façades of palazzi like the Ca' d' Oro, even public places like cafés, 'all gilded, some of them having brilliant mirrors' (Carlo Gozzi). Yes, if the Venetians had their way, they would undoubtedly have gilded all the walls of their city, inside and out. One day I saw an extraordinary piece of Venetian furniture which could not have demonstrated this better: it was a late sixteenth-century portable cabinet, in wood inlaid with painted mother-of-pearl and ivory, a technique that Venice made its speciality. Resting on a base of four steps, this edifice, with numerous columns surrounding the niches, had a sort of apse at its centre, surmounted by a half cupola. All the structures of this miniature architectural work reminded one irresistibly of the Palladium at the Olympic theatre at Vicenza and of villas along the Brenta. Now this piece of furniture was entirely covered with plaques of painted mother-of-pearl, gold arabesques and coloured flowers, while the statues in metal were of course gilded, the niches decorated inside with blue and the numerous small rings attached to the lions' muzzles (gilded obviously) which open the drawers were also gilded. Entirely Palladian, but given the gold leaf treatment. What a dream. La Serenissima completely covered in gilt, like the weather vane at the Dogana, a statue of Fortune on a gilded globe borne by two Atlantes, which, whatever way the wind blows on the Lagoon, displays the direction of riches.

Symptomatically, Venetian painters have spent more time than others, the Tuscans and the Umbrians for example, extricating themselves from all this gold, which not only covers all the backgrounds of the paintings, but, in the cases of Paolo and Lorenzo Veneziano, covers the figures with fine lace patterns of flowers, stars and geometry, themselves gilded. Venice often has the colour of money, of her ducats. And it is in such moments, when I am confronted by her ostentatious riches, that I share Lady Chatterley's aggravation when her pimp of a gondolier wanted to seduce everyone yet make them pay: 'Built of money, blossomed of money, and dead with money. The money-deadness! Money, money, money, prostitution and deadness' (D.H. Lawrence, *Lady Chatterley's Lover*). 'The petrification of capital' is how Ferdinand Braudel describes the embellishments of an enriched and prosperous Venice, which paved the streets of beaten earth and replaced the wooden quays and bridges with *fondamenta* and bridges of stone. One might equally call it the 'aurification' of the capital to describe this ostentatious desire to display this precious metal everywhere. The whole town, the *città d'oro* as Petrarch called it, exudes gold. There is a story that, at the beginning of the twentieth century, a beautiful Italian woman, a certain Marchesa V, gave fabulous costumed receptions at the Palazzo Venier, where amidst young leopards prudently injected with morphine so that they would not devour the guests, a naked pianist, painted in gold, played on his instrument. While one can certainly deplore the bad taste and vulgarity of such a 'goldfinger', one cannot contest its eminently Venetian character.

One day in his palazzo Mariano Fortuny organised a *fête de palette*. One colour was assigned to each guest. As one of these guests was particularly displeasing to the master of the house, he gave him yellow which he loathed. And it is said that the guest duly arrived in yellow, and, to the couturier's great satisfaction, suddenly fell ill and had to leave the reception in a great hurry. I am not at all surprised that Fortuny as a Venetian detested yellow, which was, interestingly, the colour of the shawl habitually worn by courtesans. The colour of venality, of arrivisme, the colour of nouveau-riche Venice. But also the colour of intolerance and of exclusion, since the Jews of the Ghetto, the first Ghetto in the world, had at first to wear it on their chest as a yellow wheel (a piece of material in the form of a small wheel), then as a beret (or a pointed or conical hat) which was also yellow (in the Middle Ages yellow was the infamous colour of madness and crime), come winter and summer, on pain of incurring a fine of fifty ducats and a penalty of a month's imprisonment.

'*Oro, oro, oro,*' the greengrocers shout at the tops of their voices in summer, all along the campiello Anconetta, as they sell passers-by their 'gold drops', those huge, very sweet, yellow plums.

∞ Inner light ∞

'The colour of Venetian painting is fine, not because it expresses a fine sensuousness but because', as the art critic Adrian Stokes wrote, 'it expresses a noble apprehension of the forms of the outside world. The strength of Venetian painting lay in those artists' humanistic power to conceive shapes as possessing their own inner light or life, in other words, colour... The light on their forms was little external to those forms. They conceived and exploited to the full a value which henceforth must always exist in European painting, the value of inner light. Instead of attempting to rival with the new-found oil paint the brilliance of specular reflections, they thought to put this specular light *behind* the surface of their pictures by painting darkly on a light ground, and by the multiple use of glazes to which oil paint lends itself' (*Colour and Form*).

It is true that in all Venetian painting the lighting seems to come from inside the canvas itself, and not from somewhere outside. But as always in the domain of painting this impression, although it seems to ring true, has a technical explanation. As the Venetians progressively explored the different possibilities offered by oil painting with its thick texture, as David Rosand shows, they would develop this medium's potential opacity more than its transparency. And from this 'a reversal of the priorities and phases of execution' would ensue. 'Instead of constructing layers of transparent pigment, the effect of which depended ultimately upon the white gesso ground, the new practice worked up from a dark base. The canvas was built up with a brown ground, a middle tone over which lights and darks were applied; the light now meant opaque white, which became the thickest part of the painting. Transparent glazes, no longer an element of the foundational structure of the painting, were reserved for subsequent modifications of hue and tone' (*Painting in Sixteenth-Century Venice*). Light was no longer an existing primary element. It now had to be introduced in order to recreate reality and make its colours stand out from the darkness that originally surrounded and obscured it.

Fading colours

It is absolutely true that sometimes in high summer or deep winter, when there is too much light or almost none, Venice can be deathly pale, divested of colour, impalpable, unreal. Murky watery mists and vague effects of dilution, powdery, ill-defined silhouettes. A blurring of shapes where only a few more precise details swim fugitively, the twin bays of a Gothic palazzo, a bit of loggia, the top of a campanile. When a diffuse sun flattens perspective, erases the differences and the details.When the winter fogs efface the buildings, make them lose their volume, reduce them to sinister greyish surfaces. Blurred decoration, uncertain geometries. This is the Venice that Emmanuel Robles evoked in a long description in *Un hiver en Venise (A Winter in Venice)*: 'Always fog, in vast layers over the town which seemed as though painted in thin faint lines on frosted glass, and wan colours from pearl grey to that green that is seen in window cracks. When night fell, this same fog even erased the burning torches of Marghera, the industrial city. When the light decomposes, all the cupolas seem to become unmoored, like those richly decorated hot-air balloons immobile in that depthless space.' While at the Lido, standing in total dereliction 'the baroque silhouette of the Hotel Excelsior took on the appearance of a ship resting on nothing in this fickle light.' This is Venice seen through windows veiled with sea spray from the vaporetti. This fluid, vaporous Venice can be seen in the many poetic, deliquescent photos taken by the predictable, repetitive Fulvio Roiter. Vague, misted silhouettes of the basilica of St Mark and the campanile, nebulous and ghostly views of the Lagoon and the vaporetti, confused façades of the palazzi along the Grand Canal, the church and monastery of San Giorgio Maggiore bleached out, softened in snow, indistinct. As though everything is crumbling. There are so many excessively aesthetic clichés which work on paradox (in the way modern photography very often does in its desperate quest for that increasingly elusive originality) in order to escape the so-called stereotypes of Venice in spring and summer, sunlit, luminous, coloured, joyous, laughing. While it may be true that Venice is in many respects a northern city where life is sometimes difficult, giving so much emphasis to strategems of indistinction and erasing out is completely contrary to the Venetian way of thinking, which strives by every means possible to resist the stresses and strains of its natural milieu, and joyfully denies its sad geographical and meteorological reality. Just take a look at the eighteenth-century *vedute* painters whose whole effort, pictorially, is to make Venice clearer and brighter. Antonio Canaletto, Luca Carlevarijs, Bernardo Bellotto, Michele Marieschi who painted souvenir views for foreign tourists, especially the rich English, that are luxurious and aristocratic equivalents of our modern democratic postcards, share a common desire for accuracy, both topographical and documentary. In the last instance, their aim is to clarify the architecture with the most extreme precision in order to protect themselves from the ambient liquefaction, to paralyse the real and to formalise the informal in order to defend themselves against the forces of dilution and the dissolution of the Lagoon. For them it is a question of objectivising Venice in order to stabilise it, solidify it, confer-ring upon it a compact and resistant consistency, inscribing it in hardness, permanence. Even the 'impressionism' of Francesco Guardi, which offered more spontaneous, more flowing, more atmospheric *vedute*, did not set out to deconstruct Venice. Symptomatically it would be painters coming from abroad, Turner and Whistler, who would cultivate these charms of a pastellist, where light eats away the architectural detail, and reduces it to transparent surfaces.

The incomparable romantic glamour of indistinctness and visual erasures return in many paintings and writings about Venice. To a point where the optic glamour of Venice paradoxically leads a number of writers to imagine what it would be like to be blind. If one is to believe this little bit of dialogue about it by Ferdinand Bac, it could be very amusing to play the blind man in the city of the doges: 'I listen to Venice. What a sensation, Monsieur. With my eyes closed, I gulp in the mystery of the town in long draughts, and I recognise it without seeing it. Isn't what one hears worth just as much as what one sees? But one hears almost nothing. Ah. This just shows how coquettish Venice is. One hears no noise, but one hears a thousand delicious noises. They do not smother one another. They complete each other, superimpose one on another, sustain one another, like a symphony. And this music sounds like a masterpiece to me. How long have you been there, choosing to play the blindman? For an hour' (*Le mystère vénetien*). Sounds rather than sights. But occasionally the blindness is real. 'On 16 January 1616,' as Philippe Jullian recounts in his biography of D'Annunzio, 'the writer-fighter left in a seaplane, and was forced by the wind to land on a sandbank. Flung by the impact against the machine-gun at his side, he completely lost his sight for several hours.' He was quickly taken to the hospital for the blind and there, half opening one eye, he came upon the horrible spectacle of soldiers with their eyes bleeding, their heads enveloped in bandages, one of whom – showing an unbearable disrespect and cruelly wounding his pathological narcissism – said to him : *Questo e quell'uomo?* – Who is this fellow?' D'Annunzio had definitely lost his right eye and there was nothing to be done there, and to save his left eye which was also very affected, the doctors told the wounded man that it was imperative that he obey two instructions: absolute darkness and absolute immobility. Gabriele D'Annunzio took refuge in the Casetta Rossa where he would be nursed by the affectionate and attentive Renata, the daughter he had had with Princess Gravina Gruyllas di Rimaccia after she had left Anguissola di San Damiano, the Neapolitan count who was her husband, to live in splendid misery with the poet at Resina, about ten kilometres or so from Naples. This Casetta Rossa, the little red house (also known as the *Casina delle Rose*, the little house with roses) which, when you take the vaporetto to St Mark's, is on the left side of the Grand Canal, between the Accademia and the Piazzetta, has hardly changed since the time D'Annunzio underwent his painful convalescence there until the end of April. It is a small palazzo ('almost a doll's house', the poet wrote, but he always exaggerated 'all red with flowers') situated between Casa Stecchini and the palazzo Corner, which seemed relatively modest in comparison with some splendid Venetian houses. In *Quatre Saisons à Venise (Four Seasons in Venice)* – and in this instance it is spring – Alain Gerber imagines the slow recuperation, interspersed with *I magnifico's* gallantries, his eyes blindfolded, dreaming of Venice. Nor was Jean Giono insensible to the charms of blindness in such a town, to the extent that he exclaimed: 'How happy a blind person would be in Venice' (*Voyage en Italie*). According to him, 'our sense of vision is always somewhat blasé, in Venice as elsewhere', while 'the ear is more sensitive because noise is hardly ever a source of delight'. If by chance sounds grow softer, our hearing possesses new intact strengths. In Venice, the discreteness of sounds, however, helps us perceive them, and makes them beautiful. 'Besides this puffing [the passage of a boat], the small cries of the magpie, the snuffling of the Turk, there is silence. The customers at the bar are as quiet and prudent as the prisoners who escaped. You can hear the sound of wine being poured into glasses, the rattle of knives and forks scraping against plates and the sizzle of oil frying on the stove, and with it additional sputtering when the shrimps are tipped in'. This is why 'the silence of Venice can be used tirelessly for pleasure (and not a banal pleasure at that) for a whole lifetime. It has, however, that quality of great silences. Ever since I disembarked (and this is the word) at the Autorimessa, I am experiencing why through the centuries so many men of quality have fled the world, which can be defined as follows: a sense which rarely is used for pleasure is *at last* being used for this purpose. There is certainly music, but it is artifice however beautiful it is. We use it like an essence. It cannot be listened to except in weak doses: an hour or two at the most.' More than a simple fantasy, this erasure of images was unfortunately a reality for Jean-Paul Sartre, when he stayed in Venice, for he was almost completely blind. Alone in his room, he listened to music on the radio. A marvellous little oasis of sound in the cultural capital of images. Beyond the mimesis and sufferings that Venice had always inflicted on him. At last serene, tuned in to the world. Blind, but listening attentively. Happy, 'in time'? But did Sartre truly love Venice once? His attitude is, to say the least, ambivalent: fascination and repulsion, attraction and disgust.

But I've said enough. Paradoxes annoy and exasperate me. It is out of the question that I continue listening to all these birds of ill omen, all these false prophets who would have someone deaf go the opera at La Fenice to fully appreciate the décor and the superb neo-rococo ornamentation of the auditorium. It is out of the question that I cede to these masochistic temptations of blindness. For 'this town is the city of the eye; your other faculties play a faint second fiddle ... the purpose of everything here is to be *seen*. In an analysis even more final, this city is a real triumph of the chordate, because the eye, our only raw, fishlike internal organ, indeed swims here: it darts, flaps, oscillates, dives, rolls up. Its exposed jelly dwells with atavistic joy on the reflected palazzi, spiky heels, gondolas etc, recognizing in the agency that brought them to the existential surface none other than itself' (Joseph Brodsky, *Watermark*).

Multi-coloured geometry:
∽ St Mark's floor ∽

Make the most of a rainy day and visit St Mark's basilica, and, once you are inside, decide never to look up throughout the whole visit. You are forbidden to look at the vaulting and the pretentious gold mosaics. Beneath your feet the basilica's sumptuous carpets of marble spread before you. A complex arrangement of the entire gamut of geometric shapes: 'Circles: in Isoceles triangles, or aligned, four circles and a smaller one in the centre, four small circles with one large one in the centre, interlocked circles. Squares: straight, at forty-five degrees, in strips as edging. Rectangles: great central compositions, carpets. Trapezoids: in semi-circular groups, on the inside of hexagons and octagons. Diabolos: in decorative bands. Cones. Triangles. Hexagons. Octagons. Checkerboard: variations. Arcades.' An unbelievable diversity of stone – specialists have identified no less than forty-four varieties: Greek white, Covolo white, White veined Carrara, White Carrara Fantastico, Statuary white Carrara, White Carrara Arabastaco, White Carrara Calacato, Bardiglietto, Travertine from Tuscany, Roman Travertine, Trani, Serpeggiante, Blue or blue-veined Turquino marble, Aurora di Brescia, Antique Red, Verona Red, Red Ramello porphyry, Carrara Red, Serpentine from Stella, Green from the Alps, Green Cypolin, Potoro, Belgian Black, African Black, Lumacchio Black, Basalt, Griggio Carnico, Dolomite, Pomarollo, Stone from Istria, Enamel, Diaspora, Jasper, Onyx from Pakistan, Green Onyx, African Onyx, Alabaster, Lapis lazuli, Aureli Emanuella, Giciello Pinatale, Rosso Rubino, Bianco Gioia, Breccia dell'Acqua Santa' (André Bruyère, *Sols. Saint-Marc, Venise – Floors. St Mark's*). Every possible and imaginable shape, and above all, every available colour of marble from all over the entire world. But when it comes to the complex and subtle geometric layout, or the multiple, changing colours, which of these elements is in the ascendancy? André Bruyère, an architect by profession, says that it is the organisation, which is so precise and so refined, that predominates, since the geometry lays down the conditions for the colours. 'The organisation is never impaired by the colours but always dizzyingly seduced by them.' It is too easy to say this, for the floors of St Mark's, that are never truly flat and horizontal, undulating as they do like a carpet or a rough sea because of the unstable boggy ground beneath the floor, worn down unevenly by the incessant tread of visitors, the varying hardness of the stones ('serpentine and porphyry stand out while the light whites have sunk, and the red marbles are halfway between the two'), cracked or well polished, pitted or smoothed, broken or eroded, these floors ensure that the materials hold their own, and ensure the play of colours against geometric programming.

Obviously Venetians in general, even the most privileged, were unable to afford such sumptuous claddings of marble to pave the floors of their own palazzi. And the *terrazzo alla veneziana*, that can be found on the *piano nobile* of so many noble Venetian dwellings, was a less expensive solution: it is a lime-based cement in which small pieces of marble have been sprinkled. The result is a sort of dispersal of colour that delighted the Venetians who love walking on colour.

I like to take an early morning stroll through the vegetable markets in Venice where they sell produce that comes from San Erasmo and Vignole, the market gardening islands of the Lagoon. Rather than the huge, famous Herbaria market near the Rialto, which has been there, in the same place, for more than ten centuries, I prefer this more modest one, which displays vegetables and fruit right the heart of Dorsoduro, on the Ponte di Pugni, just next to San Barnaba. I especially like that ponderous *peotta*, painted in red and black with a stripe of yellow; in summer it has a green awning to protect the merchandise from the fierce heat of the sun and pigeon droppings, tied at one end to the mast and at the other to a mooring post in the canal. It always occupies the same mooring along the rio di San Barnaba in front of the Ai Padovani restaurant. If you look at the way the owner takes such care, every day, to display his multi-coloured merchandise in such beautiful and regular order, you can see that his stall is a greengrocer's crude vegetable version of the marbles in St Mark's: the matt off-white cauliflowers, impeccable brilliant white onions, blood red tomatoes, red apples, with a hint of yellow jasper, orange red carrots, orange apricots, very pale, very bland yellow melons, bright yellow bananas, yellowy green plums, beige and pink dried haricots, dirty beige potatoes, tender green figs, sometimes bursting with purple, very light, brilliant green cabbages, very dark green cucumbers, with a flushing of yellow, greens, yellows and reds of peppers, raw green unripe Roman tomatoes, lettuces, marbled green watermelons, deep purple cherries, purple plums and aubergines, mauve cabbages marbled with white.

As if Venice took pleasure in giving colour to edible things. Over a century ago fruit stalls sent Théophile Gautier into ecstasy: 'There is no more enjoyable way to feast the eyes, and often, without feeling the least hungry. It has happened that we have bought some of these peaches and grapes out of pure love of the colours. We also remember certain fishmonger's stalls covered with small fish that were so white, so silvery, so mother-of-pearl that we wanted to swallow them raw for fear of spoiling their delicate colouring, like the fish-eaters of the South Seas, and it made us appreciate the barbarity of those ancient feasts, where they watched the Moray eels die in crystal containers to enjoy the opaline colours that mottled their agonised bodies'

(*Italia*). And the same Gautier remarked that on the bank of the Arsenale 'they serve you mullet from the Adriatic (*trigli*) that are so appetising, so vermillion, of such a fresh and vivacious colour, that we might only have eaten them for the pleasure of the colour, had they not been, as indeed they are, the best in the world.' In Venice colours are to be savoured.

Multi-coloured geometry:
∽ Burano's houses ∽

When, on a dreary winter morning, you take a vaporetto and cross the flat dull stretches of the Lagoon that the dim light has drained of colour, and you reach the island of Burano, you experience what can only be described as a real chromatic commotion once you have gone past the little grassy square planted with trees. For there is nothing more brightly coloured than the fishermen's very modest little houses; it is just as though as you had been transported to the Ionian Islands. The incredibly pure bright colours of the façades, English greens, geranium reds, Prussian blues, pinks, strong yellows, and deep ochres, sumptuous mauves, and even whites that explode in the heart of this intense polychromy. These stupefying juxtapositions of colour of the façades challenge all the laws of complementarity, there are multi-coloured streets where a cobalt blue is next to a turquoise green, a royal blue, a purple and a deep mauve with, on the opposite side of the street, a Pompeian red, a khaki green and a light ochre. Each dwelling is always of two or three colours in strong contrast and in rigorously geometric shapes, a combination of squares and rectangles: blue walls, green shutters, red door, or walls of light green, darker green shutters, ochre door. With frames for doors and windows that are pure white. With the roofs in the warm terra-cotta tones of orange and brown tiles. Burano's colours, however, were once upon a time distinctly less bold than they are now 'for the pigments were originally mineral:

chalk white, yellow ochre and red ochre to which had been added Treviso green, earth of an intense green which came from Monte Baldo; this pigment had a stable quality but it was too expensive for the fishermen and was only ever used in a small quantity. From 1870 onwards, a new colour appeared on the façades: Prussian blue, which had begun to be produced on an industrial scale in Germany...After the Second World War, the people of Burano began to use paints with organic pigments which would progressively give these scenes the present-day range of exceptionally rich colouring' (Jean-Philipe Lenclos). Because of the salinity which attacks and rapidly degrades these façades, they are all repainted at least every two or three years, or again at the time of religious festivals, Easter in particular. And there is a lovely legend that it was the women who painted their houses in these sparkling colours, with brushes attached to long rods, in order to help their husbands away at sea to pick out their home from afar when they wanted to return to the island.

It is good that today it is cold: the old lacemakers, always dressed in black shawls, are not making lace on their cylindrical cushions that they use to support their work as they sit outside their shops in summer, and the rare tourist sightsees very little. There is nothing that exasperates me more than all those naperies, napkins, tablecloths, embroidered blouses, for the most part made in China, apparently. Nothing drives me to despair more than lace, even authentic (by a miracle) lace, for it takes ten workers three years to complete a simple tablecloth. And in the past an elaborate piece needed seven lacemakers, each one of whom was skilled in one particular stitch. Little did it matter then that this lace was in *punto in aria*, which is the speciality of the island, *reticella*, guipure, découpé with leaves, or in scallops, knitted in squares or even rose point [Roseline stitch], the most famous of all the Venetian stitches, for, in any case, as the old Burano lacemakers say, 'You can lose your eyesight looking'. Now, in Venice, there is nothing that goes more against the grain than ruining your eyesight and not being able to see anything any more. Colour demands that you have a meal at the Trattoria di Romano Barbaro where the walls are covered with paintings by artists established on the island. For there is a school of Burano painting and even a Prize for Burano painting. As long ago as 1911 Burano's light and colour attracted the painter Umberto Poggioli, who was soon joined by Gino Rossi, Villani Marchi, Pio Semeghini and Filippo De Pisis, who came as much to forget the bitterness of repeated rejections by the Venice Biennale as to capture the dazzling polychromaticism of the island. Orazio, who now has the trattoria, has taken over his father's tradition and canvases are crammed in tight rows on the walls of the restaurant. As if it were possible, or necessary, to compete all over again with what is already done perfectly on the outside walls of the houses. A stupid gamble, doomed to failure from the start.

Today Burano is peaceful and calm, almost deserted. The brightly coloured boats have returned home. Fishermen's nets lie on the quays. Washing of every colour is hung out to dry. I take a walk in this little miniaturised and simplified Venice, just a few bridges and a few canals which reflect the little houses, usually of just one storey, or two at the most, in this Venice which is architecturally purified and chromatically surcharged. Each year I cannot stop myself from returning to Burano to discover new chromatic arrangements, which are always unexpected and surprising. For here the colours are random and ephemeral, dependent on the whim or humour of the owners, free to change the colour every time they do up their façades. And every year I revisit the San Martino church to see Giambattista Tiepolo's astonishing crucifixion 'which is like a ghastly masquerade ball, with banners and swirling draperies, and late-Goya faces, and peering deformed wretches in stage rags. The swooning virgin wears a dainty shirred morning cap and a red gown. In the background, there are clown figures in chalky grisaille, with leering swollen lips and potato noses' (Mary McCarthy, *Venus Observed*). A nerve-racking vision of anguish and terror. Mankind beaten, defeated, like the lamentably wilting Virgin in the foreground with her immense red mantle which bloodies the whole canvas, but with great chromatic discretion, multiplying the deafening, livid tones. People, frightened and terrified because of what is happening. In the mid ground are larval, ghostly faces grimacing like masks. A convulsive, grotesque carnival of grief. And what if the good Lord has abandoned us? It's just that people don't enjoy themselves every day in the isolation of Burano, for long the poorest of all the islands. So one can better understand the specifically conspiratorial value of the multi-coloured houses, the only luxury they have: how difficult it must have been and how frightening, a few centuries ago, to be so lost, so far away in the vast Lagoon.

Multi-coloured geometry:
∽ Chioggia's boats ∽

You must go to Chioggia at least once to realise that, just as on Burano, colour, in the context of the Lagoon, is existentially a life-and-death matter, a question of survival. What Burano's inhabitants have done on the walls of their houses, Chioggia fishermen have done to their *bragozzi,* their great, flat-bottomed fishing boats. You must not forget that Chioggia was a very isolated fishing centre, set between the sea and the Lagoon, and not connected to terra firma by a bridge until the twentieth century. And further that, until the end of the nineteenth century, Chioggia, in its extreme isolation in the Lagoon, was the end of the world. To get there you had to follow the Pellestrina shoreline from the Lido, that long. narrow cordon of land along which the *murazzi* run, those gigantic walls built between 1744 and 1782, under the direction of the Venetian engineer Bernardo Zendrini, to protect Venice and the Lagoon from the terrible furies of the angry Adriatic. Twenty kilometres of ramparts that are both impressive and derisory. Rising to a height of 4.5 metres above the average level of high water, vertical on the Lagoon side and sloping to a width of fourteen metres on the sea side. A Cyclopean construction with enormous stones from Istria that have been carefully tailored and cemented with a mixture of *pozzolana* and lime to which have been added blocks of marble bearing the lion of Venice. But it is impossible not to be frightened by the fragility of it all when you come upon the rusting, disintegrating carcass of that Greek cargo vessel, that a violent storm threw on to the walls at Pellestrina, where it has remained perched for many years. Furthermore, on 4 November 1966, the unleashed Adriatric inflicted spectacular damage to the walls. You must walk on this wall, on which two people barely have room to pass, to gauge the arresting contrast between the smooth mirror of the Lagoon lapping against the mud banks and the choppy surface of the sea. And the *murazzi* are also a line of chromatic demarcation, between the clearer, bluer sea and the more glaucous, greener Lagoon. 'You see,' an American friend remarks to one of the characters in Henri Sacchi's *La Dogaresse*, 'the water of the Lagoon does not have this deep warm blue of the Mediterranean, nor even that light celadon so characteristic of the Adriatic. It is the cold grey of steel, clouded in many places by the mud and seaweed suspended in it and uninviting to bathe in. However, it remains incomparably beautiful through the velvety lights that it reflects and in the architectural splendours it reaffirms.'

In the past there was nothing more spectacular than the Chioggia fishermen's *bragozzi* anchored in tight rows along the quays; their main sheets in the shape of a trapezoid and their prows marvellously ornate with decorations as naïve as they were fascinating, and whose regulated complementarity was a veritable ritual. If yellow, orange and white had been chosen for the central part of the sails, white, blue and yellow were the most frequently used colours for the lower part which is wider. The centre of the sail featured an infinite variety of heraldic emblems, both religious and secular. As you might expect, a great number had a religious content such as the crucified Christ, the Holy Virgin, patron saints. Others featured the natural world with which the fishermen had to come to terms: the compass rose, the moon and the sun. And there were many others, many more mysterious and hermetic, which were monograms, symbols or designs featuring the name of the *paron*, the owner of the boat, or members of his family, their qualities or defects. On the prows great eyes were painted (to survey the sea and chase away evildoers), stars of the sea, birds, sirens sounding the trumpet, unicorns, winged angels, St George on his warhorse killing the dragon with his sword. On the black lower part of the hull a white or reddish brown line indicated the plimsoll line. It was out of the question that a Chioggia fisherman should to take to the sea without the protection of all this superb multi-coloured geometry.

Yet Chioggia is now only a memory of its past. The *bragozzi* certainly have not disappeared but their decoration has been simplified (all that remains on the prows are some eyes and some compass roses), and motors have taken over from most of the sails. But, as a consolation, and an evocation of the ancient feasts of colour, there still remain the potbellied heavy hulls of the boats, almost invariably black below, and red and blue above the fine yellow stripe.

∽ Wintry grisailles ∽

Honoré de Balzac has left a description of his arrival in
Venice on Tuesday 14 March 1837: 'The rain cast a grey
cloak over Venice, that might have lent a poetic air to this
poor town, which everywhere is cracking and, hour by
hour, sinking, but it was rather unpleasant for this Parisian
who enjoys this mantle of mists and this tunic of rain for
two thirds of the year.' The tone is set. There will be many
texts that will wallow melancholically in subtle grisailles:
'Today, All Saints' Day, all the bells of Venice are ringing out
in a silvery grey sky, in a sky of pearl, but a lustreless pearl,
a dead pearl...' (Henri de Régnier, *L'Altana ou La Vie
vénitienne*). 'This morning there was a veiled October sky:
an opaline grey, the colour of ancient lustres that are so
fragile that you need marabout feathers to dust them' (Paul
Morand, *Venises*). And the whole of Liliana Magrini's *Carnet
vénitien*, a delicate evocation of Venice in winter, 'a
suffocating world of grey and mist', continually paints the
town in grey, a town 'which is on its own, between the grey
of the sky and the grey of the water'. A whole agreeably
detailed cameo in grey and in a variety of forms: 'solid and
compact grey' which is 'gentle on the soft brightness of the
water', when the town is seen from a little way off, 'blue
grey which is the gentle colour absorbed from the
colourless sheen of water and sky', of the water at Bacino,
'clouded with yellowish grey', the 'grey air' of a 'dirty grey
day', the 'grey arabesques of trees', the 'silky grey of
cupolas', the 'washed grey of façades', the 'dry grey' or
'translucent grey' of the sky, the 'uniform grey of the Rialto

market', the 'overall grey worked with fine white streaks' of
the city at dusk. Even the Sartrian city would also favour
grisailles: 'Venice is grey velvet. The sky grey, damp,
aqueous, grey-green water' (*La reine Albemarle ou le dernier
touriste – Queen Albemarle or the Last Tourist*). And another
lover of wintry Venice lingers over the 'stained glass in
grisaille' of the Adriatic, the 'grey hotels' of the Lido, the
'grey cotton-wool fog' (Lucien Bély, *Belle Venise*). For Jean
Raspail, as long as the sky remains low, there is nothing but
to pass from the town to its inhabitants by celebrating ' this
incomparable grey light that is like the very soul of the
Venetians' (*Vive Venise – Long Live Venice*). But, God knows,
ever since time was, the Venetians themselves particularly
detest those sinister grisailles, as Chateaubriand noted
when he visited St Mark's in 1833: 'The most remarkable
effect of its architecture is its darkness under a brilliant sky;
but today, on 10 September, the dull light from outside
harmonised with the dark basilica. We finished the
prescribed forty hours before the fine weather would return.
The fervour of the faithful, praying against rain, was great:
a grey and aqueous sky seemed like the plague to the
Venetians' (*Mémoires d'outre-tombe – Memories from Beyond
the Grave*). It is absolutely true that often in winter Venice
is *naturally* grey, 'the colour of heavy lead' as Ernest
Hemingway said. But this is precisely why this city wants to
be intrinsically artificial, why it revels in festive and
aesthetic artifice. This is why it is absurd to claim, as it
becomes more and more fashionable to do, that Venice is
more authentic, more real in winter: 'When the rains have
begun in Venice, nostalgia is so strong for the traveller there
that he must leave the town within twenty-four hours or he
will remain there like a trapped animal, dumbfounded (one
would hesitate to call it bewitched). The water of the sky
mingles with that of the canals, the world is a sponge of
stone whose narrow, streaming alveoli are barely streets
once the wind starts blowing. But then all the artificiality of

Venice disappears, everything picture postcard, all the visitor's idea of poetry. All that remains is the town in the thrall of the elements, and its people who do not know English, the beast of the Middle Ages returned to its nightmares and half dead' (Louis Aragon, *Les voyageurs de l'Impériale*). Then the travel writer multiplies the sepia effects, the sanguine lack of sparkle, the opalescence, the watercolour tones, the blurrings, as if to deaden the representation. Venice hibernates in a complacent, listless morbidity.

I have never liked angular, multi-coloured graffiti on the white façades of our French towns. And, in almost the whole of Venice, they are absent, except for one particular spot, on the long, eroded and defaced brick walls that run the length of the Fondamenta Nuove. Here I understand them, and even approve of them. For they bear witness to this determined resistance to the grey of the Lagoon, to this constant struggle against the insidious temptation to sink into colourlessness, emptiness, nothingness, without which Venice would certainly not be Venice.

∞ Iridescences ∞

There is a petrol station right at the end of the Fondamenta Nuove, on the depressing corner of the sacca della Misericordia. Just opposite – on the other side of the vast melancholy basin – the well-named Casino degli Spiriti, that the ghosts of ancient ruined gamblers must haunt each night. It is like the end of the world, like those petrol stations in the United States, in the most desolate, unpopulated places, along those interminable roads. And yet, even in these apparently disinherited spots wide open to the abyss of the Lagoon, colour will not be outdone. For here, spread out on the surface of the water, are delicate, sumptuous, moving, multi-coloured iridescences of petrol where the barges and launches fill up.

∞ Lightning flashes ∞

It is three in the afternoon on the quay at Chioggia, by the entrance to the corso del Populo. Suddenly after the superb weather we have had from early morning, the sky covers in and darkens. In a few minutes it is almost black, as if night were already falling. The souvenir pedlars hurriedly pack up their postcards, glassware, shells and model boats. The temperature drops, the wind begins to blow. And the storm bursts, violently, like a Titan. During the crossing, there are pink flashes on the Lagoon. Like those that welcomed Théophile Gautier and fired his imagination when he arrived in Venice on the night train: 'gusts of wind, squalls of rain and sudden flashes of lightning. The sky was like a basalt cupola streaked with tawny veins. On both sides, the Lagoon, with its wet blackness, blacker than pitch, stretched into the unknown. From time to time pale flashes shook their torches on the water, which was revealed in a sudden burst of flame, and the convoy seemed to leapfrog across the void like the nightmarish hippogryph, for one could distinguish neither the sky, nor the water, nor the bridge . . . The storm and the night had prepared a plate in black ink that the thunder incised in fiery streaks and the locomotive was like one of those biblical chariots whose wheels spun like flames and which snatched up some prophet into the seventh heaven' (*Italia*).

By the time I arrived at the Lido the storm had completely finished. The sun already pierced the clouds. The Lagoon had the blinding brilliance of a mirror. In the background, like Chinese shadows, the campanile and clock tower of San Giorgio, the cupolas of La Salute were clearly reflected in matt black in the water. And in a corner of the picture, the dazzling flash of a huge white liner, the *Seabourn Spirit*, moored to the Giardini. This miraculous surging of light after so much accumulated shadow was just like a Tintoretto. As one can see in the Scuola Grande di San Rocco: this literally phosphorescent saint, Mary Magdalene, surging from the sombre landscape that lies crushed under the storm-laden sky. And in observing the brutal changes of weather on the Lagoon, these phenomenal alternations of light and dark, I can readily understand that a whole part of Venetian painting has been tempted by these stormy, luminous *mises en scène* which create, for example, the whole appeal of the great dynasty of Bassanos and of the immense horde of followers who painted in the Bassanesque style.

✺ Chromatic metamorphoses ✺

After reading so many descriptions of the Lagoon by
generations of travel writers, one after the other, I have come
to recognise that it can be any possible and imaginable colour,
depending on the writer and even the mood of the same
writer. Perpetual, fabulous transformations of colour: 'The
setting sun,' wrote the nineteenth-century critic, Hippolyte
Taine, 'casts purplish tints on the Lagoon that sometimes
darken, sometimes shimmer with the ruffling of the water.
With this continuous movement all the tones are transformed
and merged. The blackish sediment or the colour of brick are
made bluer or greener by the sea that covers them; depending
on the appearance of the sky, the water itself changes, and
everything is mingled amidst streams of light, under patterns
of gold that spangle the little waves, under twists of silver that
fringe the crests of swirling water, under broad gleams and
sudden flashes that the wall of a wave throws back. The
domain and the habits of the eye are transformed and
renewed. The sense of vision encounters another world. In
place of the strong, clean, dry tints of terra firma, there is a
mirroring, a softening, a constant splendour of melting tints,
that form a second sky that is just as luminous, but more
diverse, more changing, richer and more intense than the
other, and is made up of superimposed tones that combine
harmoniously. One could spend hours watching these
gradations, these nuances, this magnificence' (*Voyage en
Italie*). Another writer, another chromatic scale: 'The water of
the Lagoon, the primary colour of which is a light green, very
similar to the colouring of the Rhine, has exactly the same

luminous qualities of matt precious stones, notably opal. The mirroring is very fluid; on the other hand, some strong lights create truly surprising reflections on the apparently flat surface. It is amazing to see that this surface, with its milky opacity, can be so sensitive to light. The sun gives it a uniformly matt brilliance from which, nevertheless, spring blinding, golden fires, in places where boats and the splash of oars stir up the water. Furthermore, the Lagoon, which was almost as flat as a mirror and motionless, was constantly animated with colours, and quite differently from on the open sea, the most lively colours never adopting the transparent lightness of sea water, but as though attenuated by a generalised milky white base, becoming more delicate, more diverse, more fugitive'(Hermann Hesse, *Travels in Italy*). And the novelist does not forget to note that 'the marshy places and the mud banks that can be recognised when the water is high by the great posts around them that indicate the navigation channels', introduce important chromatic variations in the Lagoon. 'From the boat, you can see that their colouring is different from that of the deep water; but it is from high up on the campanile of San Giorgio Maggiore, that one can observe them best, as indeed the whole Lagoon. In cloudy weather they often have a rusty colour and also a greyish dirty green; on the other hand, when the sun is shining, they appear like coloured islands with changing reflections in a Lagoon of pure green. The sun and clouds rapidly change the colour, so one experiences a particular pleasure in observing them in clear weather from the top of the clock tower. I have seen them from this place change from dull brownish red to bright carmine, the ones furthest away taking on tones that range from blue to deepest violet' (Herman Hesse). Still others see in the great mirror of the Lagoon at sunset colours of 'green bronze, ochre, deep red' (Fruttero & Lucentini, *L'amante senza fissa dimora – The Lover of no Fixed Abode*), or in the velvety dusk, tints that hesitate between colours of precious stones: 'Looking towards La

Salute, is the water lapis-lazuli, turquoise, acid blue, opal? It's a mercurial solution, whatever it is' (Philippe Sollers, *Le Coeur absolu – The Absolute Heart*). Or it becomes 'a space of pure light that, depending on the time and the season, wavers between lilac mauve, straw yellow, the whiteness of mother-of-pearl and dove grey' (Frédéric Vitoux). Or on a winter's day, 'the Lagoon is pale green seen from close by, intense blue from a distance, the opposite of mountains. Orange and violet flecks, between yellow and sepia waves, that are more or less intense depending on the depth, the sands, the wind' (Paolo Barbaro, *Lunazione veneziana – Venetian Iunations*). Or sometimes it appears like some kind of magic liquid prism 'comprising all the colours and all the tones, from purple to the reflection of the palest green silk, when it is like amber or like absinthe, with only a dash of water' (André Suarès, *Voyage du Condottiere*). The Lagoon has in it literally every colour there is. There is nothing more extraordinary than views of it from the air: the colours are made and unmade depending on the depths of the water and the currents. I myself especially like the Lagoon spread out with the colour of an aluminium plaque, lightly rippling in the wind like quivering silver.

⌘ Venetian mirrors ⌘

What does the very famous Venetian mirror generally look like? It is constructed on a wooden support, in the centre of which is a round, oval, or square mirror, which is plain and not engraved. The small plates of mirror glass that surround this are engraved by hand in the silvering (be it with a copper or stone wheel). They are then dressed with strips of coloured or transparent glass that have been twisted by hand, and fixed on with metal wire hidden by flowers or leaves, which are also made of glass, and held in place by crystal-headed nails. The main mirror is itself surrounded by mirrors. And the novelist, Michel Tournier, has taken quite an interest in this fascinating mirroring structure: 'This enormous frame is so out of proportion that it almost makes one forget the mirror itself, lost in its centre. And the frame is made up of a number of small mirrors facetted in every direction. In such a way that any feelings of complacency are out of the question. Scarcely has your eye settled on the centre, on the image of your face, than it is accosted on the right, on the left, above, below, through the secondary mirrors, which each reflect a different spectacle. It is a glancing, distracting mirror, a centrifugal mirror that chases everything that approaches its heart towards the periphery. Of course, this type of mirror is particularly revealing. But all Venetian mirrors share this centrifugal nature, even the simplest, most straightforward. The mirrors of Venice are never straight, they never return the beholder's gaze. They are oblique mirrors that oblige you to look elsewhere' (Les Météores). This is a mirror that can protect you by relieving

94

you of any narcissistic fascination: here we have a brilliant analysis of the Venetian mirror, but one that leaves me more than sceptical. For Venice is fundamentally narcissistic, never ceasing to look at itself in all its glory and splendour, like the palazzi and the churches in the water of the canals. Far from delivering you from contemplation of yourself, the Venetian mirror, a subtle panoptic, is so arranged that you can never help but look at your face. Even if you are not opposite it, it will reflect you in one way or another with the help of one of its little secondary mirrors. Whether to one side, to left or to right, a little too low or a little too high, it makes no difference: it sees you and throws your face back at you. Wherever you are in the room, one facet of the mirror will capture your reflection. It is certainly not by chance that La Serenissima, the city, above all others, of the spectacular image, progressively became the great European specialist in the manufacture of luxury mirrors. And the Frenchman Charles de Brosses was lost in admiration as he watched the incredible dexterity of the Venetian artisans: 'I have just come back from Murano where I saw them working on the manufacture of mirrors. They are not so large, nor so white as ours; but they are more transparent and less liable to have blemishes. They are not run on copper tables, as with us, but blown like bottles. It requires extremely big, robust workmen to work on these, particularly to balance those great globes of crystal in the air, that are held at the end of a long hollow metal rod which is used to blow them. With the end of his hollow rod, the workman takes a large lump of molten matter from the crucible of the furnace: this material is sticky and has the consistency of glue. By blowing into it, the workman makes a hollow globe; then, by turning it in the air and presenting it continually to the mouth of the furnace, to produce a certain amount of fusion there, while at the same time turning it very quickly, to prevent the material from cooling more quickly on one side than on another, he manages to make a long oval shape. Then another workman, with the point of a pair of scissors, made like sheep shears, that is, they spring open when you relax your grip, pierces the end of the oval. The first workman, who is holding the metal rod to which this globe is attached, turns it extremely fast, while the second gradually relaxes his grip on the scissors. In this way, the oval bowl opens entirely at one end. It is then taken off the first metal rod and then attached again through the open end to another rod which has been made for the purpose; then it is opened from the other end with the same method as has been described above. The result is a long cylinder of glass of broad diameter which is again presented to the mouth of the furnace to soften it; and when it comes out of there, all in the blink of an eye, with a single snip of the scissors, the entire length of glass is cut and swiftly spread completely flat on a copper table. Afterwards it only has to be heated again in another furnace, then polished and silvered in the ordinary way' (*Journal du voyage en Italie*). It seems that Président de Brosses, elsewhere so mocking and deprecating, was fascinated by all these complex technical operations in proportion to how much they revealed of the Venetian soul – more present in a mirror than in any other object.

∽ Lustrous bronze ∾

Once again, I went into the very modest building of the Scuola di San Giorgio degli Schiavoni. And, once again, with infinite pleasure, I came upon that dear Saint George, always just as elegant and quick-tempered on his dark warhorse, engaged in combat with the dragon to save the daughter of Aia, king of Selene, a Libyan town. It will soon be five centuries that he has been engaged in this Titanesque and audacious combat, and that he has valiantly stuck his lance into the mouth of the vile monster. There is nothing more coherent, more homogenous, than Carpaccio's chromatic scale, for example in *The Triumph of St George*: the beige of the church, the light ochre of the sun, the orange and pink of the buildings, the dark chestnut of the warhorse and the light chestnut of the defeated dragon, the yellows and reds of the Eastern clothes, the red of the saddle. Even the white of a horse on the left hand side is itself slightly ochre. In all, very few blues and greens. Once again I let myself be taken over and enveloped by the radiant lustrous bronze luminosity that emanates from the succession of nine paintings. This whole warm range of oranges, ochres, browns produces a lustrous golden atmosphere in this small room. As it happens, the etymology of the French word *mordoré* that I use to describe this warm brown with golden lustres is marvellously appropriate: *more doré*, meaning Moorish and golden. In Venice, though, one certainly would not look in the Campo dei Mori for this Moorish lustrous brown colour. If the area is so named because of its proximity to the Fondaco and houses of Arab merchants, the statues of the three turbaned Mastelli brothers, Rioba, Sandi and Afani (not forgetting the fourth which can be found on the Fondamento dei Mori, nor the man in a turban and oriental costume leading a camel on the bas-relief of the palazzo Mastelli, on the side of the rio de la Madonna dell'Orto), are sculpted in cold white stone, which is now eroded and wan-looking. If the turbans, sculpted from a harder stone, have resisted erosion better, the faces themselves are unhealthily chalky and suffering from the green sickness, disfigured by wear and tear. In any case these are Moors from Morea, that is, Levantines from the Peloponnese from which they fled because of civil wars. The Venetian Orient is to be found in Carpaccio's paintings, at least as much in their colouring as in their exotic oriental themes, figures and costumes. For I have always found these paintings in the Scuola di San Giorgio, suffused with saffron, and saffron seems to me to be much more precious and more appropriate to describe them, since the orange stigmata from the flowers of this plant are used both as an aromatic and a colourant. Yes, these canvases have spicy colours, they have the flavour of all the spices that Venice imported: saffron, paprika, turmeric, pimento, cinnamon. I have always thought these paintings are like amber, and as you know this fossilised yellow resin sometimes contains little animals, insects. When I look at Carpaccio's compositions, I have the feeling that I am discovering the Venice of long ago, marvellously preserved in them, and just slightly yellowed by the passing centuries.

Black and white:
❧ Hugo Pratt's graphic novels ❧

There is a large drawing of the façade of St Mark's basilica on a double-page spread, in black and white. Just a very brief sketch of the great architectural lines of the sacred building. And, in the foreground, there is an elegant sailor, cigarette in mouth, and the great black expanse of his cap and pea jacket. This is of course Hugo Pratt's most famous hero, Corto Maltese, shown here in *Favola di Venezia (Fable of Venice)*. There is nothing really more astonishing than St Mark's basilica rendered in black and white, deprived of the reds and greens of its marble columns, divested of all its colours and gilded mosaics. More generally there is nothing more surprising than Pratt's Venice, depicted in black and white throughout the book. And for a long time I have wondered why a Venetian like Hugo Pratt had so favoured black and white in his strip cartoon books. If, in fact, Hugo Pratt was born at the Lido di Ravenna very near Rimini (when his parents were taking a week's holiday, so it happens), he was, on his mother's side, descended from a very old Venetian family, the Zeno-Toledano, jewellers whose Jewish ancestors had to flee Toledo at the time of the Inquisition and who were converted to Catholicism in Venice. Pratt spent the first ten years of his childhood in Venice, in the area around the campo Santa Maria Formosa. If his adolescence was spent in Ethiopia and if he had, on his return to La Serenissima, to flee Venice after being arrested by the SS, it was, nonetheless, in this town that he began his career as a graphic designer, belonging to what would be called 'the Venice Group'. Afterwards there would also be Argentina, periods in Brazil, life in Genoa, then Paris. He would have a house at Grandvaux, near Lausanne, a small town house in Paris's Latin Quarter, and an apartment in Cordoba, but he would return more and more regularly to work near Venice, to the roof-terraced top floor of a house in Malamocco, a little village five kilometres from the Lido: a mythical place if ever there was, since it was the first Venetian settlement in the Lagoon that Hugo Pratt could see from his terrace. Venice would always remain his home port, the pivot of his countless trips across the world. So why did Hugo Pratt, who had long basked in Venetian colourism, prefer black and white from a distance? In fact most of his books were reprinted in colour later, having been originally designed in black and white. Also, the vast majority were never coloured by him, but by Marioliana Pasqualini, Anne Frognier, the third woman who counted in his life, and finally by Laura Battaglia, Patricia Zanotti and Cettina Novelli, who had instructions to use colour only very lightly, in pastel shades, and to respect the black and white graphic effects. Hugh Pratt can argue in vain that 'if you are a bit cunning, you can do thousands of things' in just black and white, and that what has always interested him is knowing that he could achieve it, until he could achieve it with felt tips, a brush and a pen, it is still no less true that this original denier of colour remains very problematic, until one reads the small piece of autobiographical text that opens *Favola di Venezia*. There, the illustrator tells you that as a small child of six he regularly accompanied his grandmother to the old Ghetto in Venice to visit a certain Signora Bora Levi who lived in an old house. And that, as a child, he remembered – or rather Hugo Pratt turned it into fiction – two charming little squares in this neighbourhood, the secret courtyard of the Arcanas and the courtyard of the Maltese or of the Golden Mouth. I know Venice sufficiently well to recognise immediately the Corte sconta della Arcana (a photograph of which is given in the

Preface) as the picturesque Corte Bottera, near Santi Giovanni e Paolo, with its fourteenth-century arcades and the beautiful Gothic coping of its well. Hugo Pratt rebaptised these Venetian places so that he could include them in the Ghetto. And how can one avoid mentioning the very name of Corte dei Maltese, the imaginary origin of Corto Maltese in the Ghetto? Now if there really is a neighbourhood in Venice where colour seems to have lost its right to exist, it is the enclave formed by the three parts of Venice's Ghetto: the Ghetto Novo, the Ghetto Vecchio and the Ghetto Novissimo. Go into this Ghetto through the modest doorway and the *sottoportico* which can be found on the Fondamenta della Pescheria, by the Canareggio canal. Instantly you will see the grey sadness of the façades, the lamentable flaking of faded, blistered rough cast, torn away in great patches. And instantly the extreme narrowness of the *calli*, the height of the buildings, six or seven storeys high, more like public housing than Venetian palazzi with their tiny disorderly, tightly shut windows, stifle you. The Jews, constrained by the Venetian Republic to live in an area that was more or less restricted, had no other option but to build higher and higher. It was not possible to lose a single square metre. These were the first skyscrapers. It is not only that the splendour of Venice is entirely absent from the Ghetto, but it has taken refuge inside its constructions, in the numerous synagogues, the Scuola Grande Tedesca, the Scuola Canton, the Scuola Italiana, the Scuola Levantina and the Scuola Grande Espagnola. If, undeniably, the choice of black and white made purely graphic and aesthetic decisions easier for Hugo Pratt, it is also equally true that this absence of colour echoes a melancholy that has its source in the atmosphere of the Ghetto. To understand Hugo Pratt properly, you must see that film of him rapidly drawing Corto Maltese, at least once. He begins with the sailor's cap, and his first line on the paper has, as if by chance, the exact shape, the perfect structure of a Venetian bridge. And each time he draws his favourite hero in a new posture, in a new adventure, in new settings, Hugo Pratt is noting him down in Venetian topography. No matter where he is in the wide world, in Ethiopia or in Siberia, he is still in Venice.

Black and white:
∽ Shadows and lights ∽

Despite the undisputed predominance of colour, Venice can still apparently produce extraordinary effects 'in blackness and whiteness: water brings commerce between them. Italians excel in the use of black and white, white stone and interior darkness. Colour comes between, comes out of them, intensely yet gradually amassed, like a gondola between water and sky.' So Adrian Stokes remarked in *Venice*. And his whole book is an admirable analysis of these complex, quasi-dialectic links between black and white, which create and intensify each other, particularly because Istrian marble, used on such a massive scale in Venice, 'blackens in the shade…bleaches in the light' preserving, dramatising, bringing about the play of shadow and light: the white frames of the windows are adjacent to the extreme darkness of the interiors, but in return 'the darkest windows obtain a kind of radiance from the fact of aperture above the closed waters: their darkness burns slowly and forever over the reflecting element that is partly dark and partly light.' There would be therefore no more exemplary image of Venice than 'the five blackening balustrade-supports to the last window of the old prisons [that] have white swelling breasts. They are like penguins. The black and white of sea-birds are stones in Venice.' So must we conclude that in essence and depending on the colour itself, 'columns and projections on Venetian buildings are most dramatically light and dark' possibly because they are built in a stone which possesses the curious optical property of whitening the light and darkening the shadow. In fact, Adrian Stokes, who knows that he cannot endlessly sustain his subtle paradox is himself obliged to agree that ' in Venice, as a whole, tone so easily acquires these values ascribed to colour. Thus blackness, as well as whiteness, obtains a meaning over and above its tone value, more especially that value fundamental to profound colour relationship, identity in difference. The gondolier's seaworthy serpent . . . is black between water and sky: but rather than as a silhouette whose character is to stand out, and the character of whose background is thus to be a contrasting background, the black gondola appears in organic connexion, suggestive of circulation, which belongs to colour rather than to tone. This solid blackness seems to have been extracted from the dark places of water which therefore now appear lighter.' This is an absolute triumph of chromatic aberration. In Venice, even black and white succeed in re-entering the colour spectrum, but reciprocally colours do not completely escape a black and white effect. Thus raising this comment on the campo San Zan Degola: 'An extreme degree of discolouration in a town of washed out colour. But nothing lacklustre, rather a diffuse luminosity, subtle passages of light and shade which veil or unveil a pale sun, as would movement on a naked body.

'The square is empty at this time in early afternoon; nothing makes a spectacle except the tiny, slow metamorphosis of colour when the eye moves from one subject to another... The nuances between flesh and stone in the campo seem to be situated in a no-man's-land of the solar spectrum: photographed in black and white, the space would lose what the white secretly contains of pink, yellow and grey. Photographed in colour, it would appear like a black and white photo' (Edwige Lambert, 'Le grain de la vue – The scrap of view').

Black and white:
∽ Old photographs ∽

Take time to browse through one of the many books of black
and white photographs of Venice, published in the second
half of the nineteenth century and the beginning of the
twentieth. And immediately the town will seem incredibly
sinister and disturbing. In black and white, Venice is not so
much picturesque as lugubrious and seedy. There is a superb
shot by Carlo Naya: on the dark water of the Grand Canal,
in front of the Rialto Bridge, is the very black reflection of a
black gondola. A Venice in mourning. Without the warm red
glow of their brick walls that erosion constantly revitalises,
rekindles and brightens, the façades of the palazzi are
sordidly rundown. The narrow *calli* appear like miserable
alleyways of the worst of working-class districts. Sometimes
even the canals end up looking like sewers open to the sky.
Venice without colour is dead and deadly.

One day in a junk shop I unearthed two old souvenir
albums, *Venezia. 64 Vedute* and *Ricordo di Venezia* published
by A. Scrocchi of Milan, which were made up of a series of
postcards, like an accordion, in the kitschest of covers, a
Bridge of Sighs and a St Mark's Basilica in garish colours
surrounded by a garland of flowers. Some amiable pigeons
were perched, as they should be, on the (obviously) gilded V
of Venice. When I opened one of the albums two tickets fell
out, one red and the other green, *Biglietto d'Ingresso, Prezzo
Ridotto,* from the Commune of Venice, the first worth 5 lire
and the second 1 lira. Both were dated 4 August 1936, the day

when a tourist, whom I had never met, had visited a number of monuments unknown to me, and had taken the trouble each time to slip the little ticket into his book in order not to lose it. In fact nothing could have been more sinister than these two albums, one in sepia and the other in black and white, in which the gondolas still had *felze* (cabins). If one ended with a 'poetic view' of the Grand Canal by moonlight, the other, resolutely modernist, finished with views of the station, of the piazzale Roma (accompanied by the comment that 'This square will shortly become the busiest centre of Venice, above all because of the great garage under construction') and finally of the new bridge for cars over the Lagoon (which had just been opened on 15 April 1933). This Venice, in some ways so similar in essence to the one I know (even if the Giudecca canal was still a proper port then, to judge by the importance of the number of ships moored on both sides of the quays), becomes like a mortuary when to the total absence of colour is added the early 1930s' fashion of women in cloche hats. Now, when an increasing and systematic use of colour makes me so angry when it comes to old black and white movies, I have reached a state of wishing that every representation of Venice should be, obligatorily, in colour. I should add that, that day in the junk shop, I had in fact found three albums altogether, coming I expect from the same trip to Italy by the same tourist: the two of Venice were accompanied by a book on the *Camposanto di Genova. 40 Vedute,* opening with a desperate *Panorama generale del Camposanto di Staglieno,* followed by a collection of graveyard statuary whose exuberant baroque bad taste could hardly allow me to forget its function . . .

∞ African black ∞

A large poster was stuck just about everywhere on the red
walls of Venice. A seductive, sporty-looking white woman in
a bathing suit, in a canoe. She was holding a pole in her hand.
In front of her was a superb, athletic black man with ritual
scarring on his muscular body. It was of course an ad for
bathing suits. Had the modern admen of this enticing poster
known that they were reviving a very old Venetian tradition?
Black and white. This trenchant opposition of colours and
races was a constant part of social life and the arts in Venice
where every moneyed nobleman had to have in his service a
'negro' or a 'negress'. This is what Renata in Ernest
Hemingway's *Across the river and into the Trees*, reminds her
lover of, when passing the illuminated window of a jeweller's,
he asks her what piece of jewellery she would like: ' That small
Negro with the ebony face and the turban made of chip
diamonds with the small ruby on the crown of the turban. I
should wear it as a pin. Everybody wore them in the old days
in this city, and the faces were those of their confidential
servants.' In the nineteenth century it was still *'bon ton'* in the
rich aristocratic families to have a black gondolier dressed in
gaudy colours, like that 'muscular negro' who retained the
attention of the Goncourt brothers, ' with a red turban, a
white twisted string and tassel, tassels with bells around his
neck, a dark doublet brightened up with slashes, black and
white chequered shorts with blue tights' (*L'Italie d'hier – Italy
of Yesterday*). At the beginning of the twentieth century, King
Don Carlos of Bourbon, in exile in Venice, had a black servant
with red livery in his service, to drive his steam launch flying

the royal Spanish flag on the poop. One should always mistrust fiction when one reads in *L'Amante senza fissa dimora* that still, when the twentieth century was in full swing, there were certain people in the best Venetian society who (in order to preserve tradition) had blacks on their staff. So the Contessa Cosima employs two Moors for her official receptions, who because they belonged to tribes that were mortal enemies, the one being a Shoan Ethiopian, the other a Mijourtan Somalian, had a tendency to quarrel constantly and cause terrible damage. On the other hand is it certain that that great lover of disguise, the Count Emile Targhetta d'Audiffret (a real count, in no way fictitious) who lived in the palazzo Merati on the corner of the rio dei Mendicanti on the Fondamenta Nuove, employed a faithful servant of Ethiopian origin by the name of Michele? As for me, on a more modest and more democratic scale, occasionally I like to go looking for these blacks in Venice, by having a coffee in one of the two Florian's, painted with frescoes by Casa in the exotic taste of the nineteenth century. Amidst the mannerist grotesques and Pompadour decoration by Pacutti, and among other less scantily clad orientals and Turkish girls, is a black woman whose naked breasts are revealed in all their perfection. All she has to preserve her modesty is her black skin. And if a coffee at Florian's does not seem to you to be a worthwhile investment, you can simply admire, in an antique dealer's window, a negro candle-holder with a glass shade. There are still traces everywhere in Venice of an immoderate taste for these torchères. You will find two very fine ones permanently in place in campo San Barnaba, on two sides of the entrance to a wood carver's shop, near the white façade of the church. Turbans and gilded twisted belts, gilded scarf, gilded bracelet. Beige jerkin, blue blouse for one, and pink for the other. Gypsy trousers and Turkish slippers. They both carry a torchère in the shape of a horn of plenty, one of which is decorated with a lustre.

There are a great many Venetian paintings that prominently

feature a black servant, who beyond his sociological trueness to life possessed an invaluable advantage of providing the artist with superb chromatic effects. There is Pietro Longhi's *The Ambassador of the Moor* (at Ca' Rezzonico): a black servant, dressed in a fabulous crimson costume edged with white fur and wearing an astonishing hat of the same fur, bears a letter to two young women. This is also why all self-respecting historical fiction about Venice must, *de rigueur,* have a black male or female servant, for example, the gracious black woman with 'her dress of many-coloured flowers' who carries out the four wishes of the beautiful Beatrice Loredano in Alfred de Musset's *Le Fils du Titien,* or there is the Nubian 'dressed in white silk' who steers the gondola of Imperia, the seductive courtesan, in Michel Zévaco's *Les Amants de Venise.* Nor can anything be more extraordinary than this *mise en scène* which uses the contrast of white and black than the colossal mausoleum of the doge, Giovanni Pesaro, at Santa Maria Gloriosa dei Frari. This most illustrious Pesaro family, who, despite their fame only ever had one doge, decided to mark the occasion. It is an imposing monument, two storeys high, with the doge atop nobly haranguing the crowd and seated under a rich baldaquin of red marble imitating a brocade curtain. Below four pedestals in marble, decorated with festoons, uphold four gigantic Moors sculpted by Melchiorre Barthel of Dresden, porters loaded with heavy sacks on their shoulders, who serve to support the entablature. While their clothes are in white marble, in contrast, the visible parts of their bodies, their faces, arms, legs, and knees showing through torn pantaloons, are a beautiful shiny black marble. When he visited Venice, Mark Twain laughed at this funerary monument and its four Nubians: a grotesque and megalomaniac mausoleum. No matter, in Venice black is always fashionable. And Mark Twain, although he acknowledged it with his American humour, seemed somewhat vexed, mortified by his lack of knowledge of the history of Renaissance art in the company of his particularly competent guide, who, as it happens, was 'a cultivated negro, the offspring of a South Carolina slave' (*The Innocents Abroad*).

⌘ Coffin black ⌘

If there is one repetitive refrain that runs through the entire literature devoted to Venice, it is that the forever doleful gondolas are, when all is said and done, just grim-looking hearses. And here is a little anthology (obviously very incomplete) in chronological order.

Goethe: 'This gondola is like a cradle, gently sleeping
And the cabin placed upon it a spacious coffin.
And so it is. Floating and fluctuating between a cradle and a coffin,
Heedless, we pass along the Grand Canal, across this life.'
(*Venetian Epigrams*, 1790)

Chateaubriand: 'These famous, totally black gondolas have the appearance of boats that carry coffins. I took the first that I saw for a corpse being brought on land' (*Letter to Bertin*, from Trieste, 30 July 1806).

Madame de Staël, taking up Goethe's comment which she had read in Germany, very precisely: 'These black gondolas which glide along the canals seem like coffins or cradles in the last and first hours of man's life. In the evening, all one sees passing are the reflections of the lanterns which light the gondolas, for by night, being black, they are indistinguishable. You could say that they were shades gliding on the water, guided by a little star' (*Corinne ou l'Italie*, 1807).

Mark Twain: 'We reached Venice at eight in the evening and entered a hearse belonging to the Grand Hotel d'Europe. At any rate it was more like a hearse than any thing else, though to speak by the card it was a gondola...This, the famed gondola, and this the gorgeous gondolier – the one was an inky old canoe with a sable hearse-body clapped onto the middle of it, the other a mangy, bare-footed guttersnipe, with a portion of his raiment on exhibition which should have been sacred from public scrutiny' (*The Innocents Abroad*).

Richard Wagner: 'The appearance of the gondola itself was frightening; for, when I had to enter under the roof of black drapes I thought for a moment that I was part of a convoy of corpses in a Plague epidemic' (*My Life*, 1870-4).

Pierre Loti: 'At the quay by the station, I got into one of those black gondolas, enclosed like a sarcophagus, that one can hire here just like hiring a carriage...When by chance, a little way off, near the approach to some dark crossroad, there could be heard the cadenced sound of oars, my gondolier let out a long warning cry, which echoed between the damp marble walls – these streets with no passers-by have a sound system like caves – someone invisible replied, and soon another gondola appeared, as black and enclosed as mine; the two sarcophagi passed each other according to fixed rules, the one sliding past the other without touching...' (*L'exilée*, 1893).

André Suarès: 'The gondola, all the same, is just a small coffin on the sea. I have a certainty of danger that I long for: the certainty that at last I have left this world' (*Voyage du Condottiere – Vers Venise*, 1910).

Thomas Mann: 'Can there be anyone who has not had to overcome a fleeting sense of dread, a secret shudder of uneasiness, on stepping for the first time or after a long interval of years into a Venetian gondola? How strange a vehicle it is, coming down unchanged from times of old romance, and so characteristically black, the way no other thing is black except a coffin – a vehicle evoking lawless adventures at night in the plashing stillness of night, and still more strongly evoking death itself, the bier, the dark obsequies, the last silent journey! And has it been observed that the seat of such a boat, that armchair with its coffin-black lacquer and dull black upholstery, is the softest, the most voluptuous, most enervating seat in the world' (*Death in Venice*, 1912, trans. David Luke).

Jean-Louis Vaudoyer: frozen shrouds 'cunningly insinuate themselves into the bends of the alleyways and small canals and make it compulsory for gondolas to be covered with a *felze*, a box that looks like a coffin' (*Les Délices d'Italie*, 1924).

Jean-Paul Sartre: 'A gondola silently passes beneath the bridge over which I am leaning: inside is the great slumping body of an American, lying flatter than if he were dead' (*La Reine Albemarle ou le dernier touriste*, 1991).

Alain Gerber: 'Renata remarked that the gondolas looked like the hearses of our lost pleasures' (*Quatre saisons à Venise*, 1996).

Not to mention the 'small catafalques' (Mme Malibran), the 'happiness coffin' (André Fraigneau), 'funeral seahorses' (Olivier Frébourg). But enough is enough. What grave obstinacy. That constant desire to plunge into mourning for Dead Venice. In the Venetian mind, however, this black has absolutely nothing funereal about it. In 1633 the Republic passed Sumptuary Laws to restrain the increasing luxury and excessive decoration of gondolas: henceforward they had to be painted plain black. It is true, I do concede, that when the Venetian gondola still had the *felze*, a sort of small cabin with a roof shaped like a half-barrel, and with narrow windows as a protection against sea spray and bad weather, which were removed in summertime, it really did, at that particular time, look like a sort of hearse. In any case, the gondola had ardent admirers and fierce detractors among the *forestieri*. I shall not choose between them. Nevertheless dare I say simply that after all the many times I have stayed in Venice I have still never been in a gondola, unless standing, for a simple trip, from one side of the Grand Canal to the other. Has this been out of a fear of ridicule of getting into these 'seesaws for cretins' as the Italian Futurist Marinetti wickedly called them? Or out of extreme denial of all sentimentality? I cannot say that I like the sentimental exhibitionism which is given free rein, those all too public amorous urges and outpourings.. The 'only thing the locals never do, ' Joseph Brodsky remarks, 'is ride in a gondola. To begin with, a gondola ride is pricey. Only foreign tourists, and well-off ones at that, can afford it. That's what explains the median age of gondola passengers: a septuagenarian can shell out one-tenth of a schoolteacher's salary without wincing. The sight of these decrepit Romeos and their rickety Juliets is invariably sad and embarrassing, not to say ghastly. For the youth, i.e. for those for whom this sort of thing would be appropriate, a gondola is as far out of reach as a five-star' (*Watermark*). And yet the brilliant black of the gondola does tempt me. It represents supreme elegance to Venetians who have always liked and still like dressing in black (still when Jean Giono was in Venice, in the 1950s, though in the last thirty or forty years, the Venetian identity has considerably changed). 'The position of this town surrounded by water and with streets of water means that it is the only place in the world where one can wear black indefinitely and where the black remains pure. Trousers, shirt and sandals in pure black make an admirable outfit. Nothing is more cheerful. Here they make a sort of straw hat that is varnished black, with a flat crown and wide brim, brightened up with a tiny plait of green ribbon which hangs behind like a tress of twisted hair. One goes everywhere in this get-up. As there is never any dust, nothing is more economical than black. A man in black seeking his fortune is very good-looking' (*Voyage en Italie*). To the extrent that Jean Giono thought that, in Venice, black was 'the only colour *which brings something new*. The others, in the long run, become boring by repeating what the sun has already told you; which is hard to digest.' Amongst all those chromatic variations of town and

Lagoon, only black can be a colourful diversion. And it is true that when a coloured gondola crosses the shimmering Lagoon, in bright red or Prussian blue or emerald green, like a competition boat which belongs to a sailing club in Burano or San Erasmo, it strikes one as far less specifically Venetian, sometimes one is even tempted to see it as a real lack of taste. If I happen to be near the Sartorio bridge that crosses the rio de l'Arvorgaria, early in the morning, and I see, under the brick hangars in the Daniele Bonaldo boatyard (one of the last five *squeri* still in existence in Venice) a gondola that has not yet been painted, and is still completely white, to me it is just as though it has not yet removed its nightdress, and is vaguely indecent, if not to say obscene.

∞ Mud black ∞

'At the entrance to the fire station at San Polo . . . there is a large naïf painting in colour placed on an easel. A horizontal line representing the water level cuts it into two equal parts, and it illustrates life above the Lagoon (the Doge's palace, campanile, piazzetta) and life under water: there is the dense forest of piles that support the buildings, the grey or greenish undulations of sand and mud, the rotting carcase of a sunken ship, octopuses, different kinds of fish, hairy banks of seaweed, sea currents in pale blue filaments. No sign of any fire or fireplace on the surface, simply the peril of the water, as if the firemen's priority were to save Venice from being shipwrecked, and its stonework from being swamped in the Lagoon' (Brice Matthieussent). What is really disquieting is below, in the depths, under the gloomy surface of the canals. Beneath the sluggish, almost congealed, heavy and opaque water is a dark mirror of stagnant lead.

At low tide, when some of the innermost canals are almost empty, Venice is a depressing spectacle. There is a disgusting, blackish, heavy, nauseous sludge. And all those dead rats. And all that washed up detritus: Cola-Cola cans, plastic bottles, buckled saucepans. Rich and poor behave in exactly the same way in this regard: they all throw rubbish from their windows into the canals. And the canals nowadays are only rarely cleaned, unlike as was the case for more than ten centuries when they were cleaned every ten years. Now they silt up. 'The decay can be read like an open book. The water no longer "breathes" normally, that is, instead of flowing with the tide between the bases of the buildings, it lingers in their foundations, gnawing away at the sealants and the bricks used as filling, so that, one by one, they crumble and fall' (Jean Raspail, *Vive Venise*). More than anyone else, Jean-Paul Sartre, as a good Existentialist, whose invention of Bouville [literally: Mudtown, the setting for his novel *La Nausée*] always accompanied him, was all too aware of this viscous subterranean, miry and pustulent Venice, of this kingdom of erosion, corruption and decomposition, in these explicitly repugnant and nauseous lower depths. It was a cancer, a suppurating wound: 'The green water has something akin to an intestinal infection, it stinks and hides bubbles which, at twenty a second, rise to burst on the surface as if emerging from a rotting belly' (*La Reine Albemarle ou le dernier touriste*). He has more to say: 'Water becomes sordid and in Venice you can smell it. You are riding around on something disgusting, on the soft shell of a pustular beast'. Sometimes I even imagine that the blackness of Hell – in the great mosaic of the Last Judgment, on the inside wall of Torcello cathedral's façade – where the dismembered bodies of the damned, skulls with eye sockets invaded by young snakes, dismembered hands and feet, squelch about, is nothing more than the disgusting blackened and morbid mud of the Lagoon. Think of those noxious miasmas of Lagoon and canal water in the Middle Ages – putrid, repugnant, putrescent and stinking sewers, must have only nurtured the propagation of epidemics, in particular the sickness feared more than all others, more yet than malaria: the Black Death.

There is no main sewer in Venice. All the houses are constructed with septic tanks, the *pozzi neri* (black wells) whose contents cannot overflow directly into the canals and which must periodically be emptied. A whole shitty subterranean Venice supports – and threatens constantly to suck in, and swallow up – sublime artistic Venice. Sometimes in a fish restaurant on the Rialto side of the canal, I happen to eat *seppie al nero*, squid cut into thin strips and cooked in the black ink from their little sacs, often accompanied with rice which soaks up the juice during the twenty minutes of cooking and turns black. And every time I ask myself why I have chosen this dish, with its rather bitter and very iodine flavour, which does nothing for me. If I cannot stop ordering these squid quite regularly, it is because I am not there to savour one of La Serenissima's culinary specialities but rather to consume a disturbing, murky colour, the very colour of the muddy depths of the Lagoon. Now I am eating Venice itself, down to its very sediment.

❧ Ink black ❧

'Venice's canals are as black as ink', Paul Morand wrote, and went on to elaborate: 'the ink of Jean-Jacques, of Chateaubriand, of Barrès, of Proust; dipping your pen there is more than French homework, it is quite simply a duty' (*Venises*). Venice's fascinating intertextuality is made up not only from its inhabitants, its architecture, its canals and works of art, but also from all the literature that it has inspired in uninterrupted continuity down the centuries. La Serenissima is as much read about as it is wandered through, leafed through as much as it is visited. And I always like paying a visit to that enigmatic statue, perched on a brick garden wall, along the Zattere, near the rio San Vio. It is of a child presenting passersby with an open book, now blackened with dirt and moss, its head held to one side. I do not know the precise symbolic significance of this mysterious statue and its dreamy, melancholic gaze, but I have always thought that it perhaps means that Venice is visited like an open book (even if one has to look away from the page all the time so as not to neglect reality), that here the library is inseparable from the city. Some miserable people would of course be tempted to think that this surfeit of acquisitions from books runs the constant risk of killing real life for the sake of writing that is too prolix, too talkative, too facile and too verbose, as well as frequently sentimental. As Ferdinand Bac has remarked, the visitor to Venice is 'victim of too abundant a literature'. Venice, a possible 'nightmare of literature', seems to dread Henry James sometimes, who wrote so much about La Serenissima. And in fact there are moments where one can feel followed, hunted down by the shades of so many illustrious writers. It is impossible to take a single step in Venice without encountering one of them. Alfred de Musset and George Sand, and later Marcel Proust at the Hotel Danieli on the Riva dei Schiavoni, John Ruskin, lodging on the Zattere. Henri de Régnier pacing up and down that same Zattere almost daily before returning to the Palazzo Venier or the Ca' Dario, or later the 'mezzanino' in Palazzo Vendramin ai Carmini. Nietzsche was installed at the Palazzo Berlendis on the Fondamenta Nuove, Maurice Barrès lived on the Fondamenta Bragadin, near the rio San Trovaso and his gondola boatyard, Rainer Maria Rilke lodged in the 'mezzanino' of Palazzo Valmarana. Ezra Pound prowled under the tunnels of the garden of the Locanda Montin that artists and intellectuals continue to frequent. Frederick Rolfe, otherwise known as Baron Corvo, regularly squatted in the buildings of San Giorgio Maggiore. Jean-Paul Sartre wrote on Tintoretto at the Scuola di San Rocco and at the Madonna dell' Orto. If you stop for a while at the Café Florian to have a coffee, all those familiars of the place, at the turn of the last century, press all around you, till you feel suffocated by them: Henri de Régnier, Jean-Louis Vaudoyer, Jean-Paul Toulet, Claude Farrère, Abel Bonnard and many others. Useless to flee the islands. Ernest Hemingway, who occasionally decided to leave Harry's Bar or the bar at the Gritti, is ready and waiting for you on Torcello, at the Locanda Cipriani. While Lord Byron, if he is not in Palazzo Mocenigo on the Grand Canal, is resting at San Lazzaro degli Armeni or galloping along the beach of the Lido. Venice is no longer a town, but a literary anthology, where at certain moments you feel almost pursued by these ghosts of so many famous writers. So not a single place in Venice exists where there is not some repository of writing. It is useless in this situation to expect a fresh vision, or fresh intuitions.

Venice is one of those privileged places that prove that life and literature are a single entity. How can you separate the vibrant life on the *campielli* from Goldoni's comedies? How can you separate the dungeons of the Doge's Palace from Casanova's tale of his escape? And on Murano, how can you forget his gallant adventure with a nun? Have you already noticed that, in Venice, reputed to be the city of lovers, there are very few graffiti scratched into the stone or written in indelible felt-tip? Happily (unlike Verona, for example, where you can never get away from Romeo and Juliet) only rarely are there those odious hearts pierced by an arrow, with two first names and a date. Perhaps it is because the whole town is already a text, and it seems useless to add anything further.

❦ Parrot feathers ❦

How strange and unexpected, indeed almost incongruous, to find a parrot amongst the plants and foliage in front of the low marble platform on which the six saints are standing in Vittore Carpaccio's painting *I Santi Giacomo, Antonio Abate, Andrea, Domenico, Lorenzo e Nicola di Bari* (Bergamo, Accademia Carrara): the bird's breast feathers are all red, then yellow, green and blue towards the tail. It is as out of place in a sacred painting as the huge gherkins that feature in so many religious paintings by Carlo Crivelli. Also by Vittore Carpaccio is the elegant bright red parrot pecking at a plant in the foreground of *St George baptising the Gentiles*, at the Scuola di San Giorgio degli Schiavoni. And yet again Carpaccio has a parrot which features in the *Visitation* at the Museo Correr. All these parrots have been used not so much for iconographic purposes (even if, like the camel, they display a very Venetian taste for the exotic), as for a strictly chromatic reason: it is as though the painter wanted to use this spectacular multi-coloured bird as his colour chart, his palette in the painting itself, for he flaunts colour. Right in the foreground of Veronese's *Feast in the House of Levi* at the Accademia, a dwarf jester in red and orange is holding a green parrot. And at the Villa Maser, Veronese has painted a dear little parrot with a yellow head and green plumage, perched on the balustrade beside the imposing wife of Marcantonio Barbaro and the nurse, and looking towards the back of the room. In the ballroom of Villa Pisani, Giambattista Tiepolo has another one. Perched high up in the moulding of a column, on the cornice in the fresco of

Apollo and the Four Continents, there is a parrot with a very long tail, which dazzles with so many colours: a superb red plumage, highlighted in yellow, orange and blue. And yet again by Giambattista Tiepolo, there is a sumptuous red and bluey green parrot that a seductive young girl is holding against her naked breast. (Oxford, Ashmolean Museum). Tiepolo liked to export his Venetian parrots when he was working abroad. So we have a parrot featuring at the Würzburg residence, a magnificent parrot with fabulously rich colouring: a yellow beak and white head, bright red body feathers, wing feathers in orange, greens and blues, red tail feathers. A whole flight of multi-coloured parrots swoop down on Venetian painting. Not to mention the glass parrot created by Fulvio Bianconi, in 1954, for the Venini factory: this is in white lattima glass with polychromatic filaments, its beak and feet in yellow, and its plumage in red, yellow and green pastilles. Not to mention either (for the rest you will never know as it would take several days to tell), that tiny ravishing red and green parrot that is tattooed on the shoulder of a pretty young barmaid working near the piazza San Bartolomeo.

⬱ Reflections ⬰

There is probably no need to remind you that, in Venice, the reflection is a subtle modality of colour. It is a sort of fourth dimension of colour – its vibrant, transformational version. Not just the reflection of palazzi and churches in the water of the canals, but the reflections of water on façades and inside the rooms of houses. A continual *chasse-croisé*. Incessantly quivering mirrorings of the façades on the *rii*. Perpetually shimmering and glimmering of lights and shadows on the brick walls. The water's surface fragments into an infinity of small facets, enacting an abstract decomposition, like cubism, of the palazzi and churches which are broken and recomposed by the movements of ripples, refracted and diffracted with the eddies, wrinkled and spread, separated and reformed to the rhythm of the wavelets. 'Wherever you go, if you look down, you see an upside-down town in a sky more luminous than the real sky; if you look up, you see glimmers and sparkles running across the fronts of palazzi, which are no longer of marble and brick, but of a magical material, where dreams, paintings are born. All is painting in this physical, metaphysical land, all is a painter's dream, even the most solid and massive architecture, even your own body of flesh and bone' (Diego Valeri, *Guida sentimentale di Venezia*).

In fact, it is not simply the water reflecting the infinite, precarious splitting of fragile, trembling pieces of architecture, sparkling in the sun: its wavering mirrorings are reflected even on the insides of buildings, on the walls and ceilings that sail between two waters. If you visit the church of the Gesuiti, on a fine sunny day towards eleven o'clock in the morning, look at the top of the immense, heavy, marble baldaquin surmounting the main altar; it is run through with perpetual undulations and slight quiverings of light. In fact, the sunlight is reflected, waveringly, by the water of a canal, through a window just behind the altar, and refracted and dispersed, fluttering and blinking, on to the voluptuous mouldings of the polychrome marble, which shivers and palpitates. When a motor boat passes down the small canal, the agitation of the water makes the moving reflections even more rapid and frenetic. Ephemeral leaping patches animate and convulse the old marble, which loses its noble impassivity. Pirouettes of weightless matter, as it begins joyfully to dance.

↬ Pink ↫

'Asked what might be the leading colour in the Venetian concert, we should inveterately say Pink, and yet without remembering, after all, that this elegant hue occurs very often. It is a faint pink, shimmering, airy, watery pink; the bright sea seems flush with it and the pale, whiteish green of Lagoon and canal drink it in. There is indeed a great deal of very evident brickwork, which is never fresh nor loud in colour, but always burnt out, as it were, always exquisitely mild' (Henry James, *Italian Hours*). In fact in Venice there are numerous walls of old palazzi or simple dwellings covered with a gentle pink rough cast. Sometimes it is the original colour, more often these are antique Pompeian reds that have become worn, washed out, faded in sunlight and by the passage of time. 'The façades pink rough cast / Is a ghost of colour / That, beneath its pallor, ill-conceals / The dull gaps of cracks' (Jean-Louis Vaudoyer, *Les Délices d'Italie*). In La Serenissima, incessantly haunted by its glorious past, even colour, more often than not, is only a ghost of itself. There is a whole subtle scale of discolouration – dark ochres of façades have yellowed, diaphanous greens grown pale and translucid, there are uncertain blues on many of the boats. There are days when even the water loses all its transparency and becomes no more than a shadow of itself. I remember when I arrived in Venice once, just before the Christmas holiday, when the Lagoon, over which the train was travelling, seemed to be made of thick, muddy, ponderous water: it was then a strange salmon pink, a pink which was not clear, but dirty and debased, with glints of lighter pink, sparkling on the crests of innumerable wavelets that looked almost motionless in their process of constant renewal. But all Venetian pinks are not so ethereal, nor so shifting. Take the pink of octopuses spread out in the morning on the fishmongers' stalls in the shade of the great portico of the Pescaria. This delicate pink flesh did not really tempt Jean-Louis Vaudoyer: 'You must undoubtedly be an older Venetian if you are to enjoy eating those deformed pink beasts, whose appearance would not be so repellent were they not edible. These little round-bodied octopuses, the size of an egg, appear as though sculpted in red coral. They are piled up in earthenware vats the inside of which is glazed with a pale enamel mottled in dark green. It is made to look attractive to the painter, but the gourmand is less seduced' (*Les Délices d'Italie*). That pale pink can be seen again, on the heavy barges loaded with vegetables and fruit, encircled in a fine green rind, in melons called *cocomeri*, cut in two for display, that the very same Jean-Louis Vaudoyer would not like either, as if pink were decidedly inedible: 'They are oval, their skin has the blackish glistening green of certain marbles, and if you cut them, you discover a brilliant soft flesh, on which the jet-black seeds look just like the carnival masks on silk dominos'. Unfortunately their deceptive flavour far from equals the pictorial perfection of their dress: this beautiful pink flesh 'tastes like marsh, tasteless at first, bitter afterwards' (*Les Délices d'Italie*). Perhaps Jean-Louis Vaudoyer would have changed his mind on the gustatory virtues of pink had he had occasion to drink a 'Tiziano', a cocktail that is served these days in Harry's Bar. It is a delicious mixture of grapefruit juice and Champagne, coloured pink with bitters or pomegranate juice. In Venice I like drinking pink, which anywhere else I would loathe.

∽ Tiepolo pink ∽

More than once in *In Remembrance of Times Past*, Marcel
Proust returns to Tiepolo pink, a colour that visibly seduced
him, ravished him. Take, for instance, when, in the presence
of Mme Swann, the narrator protests that no 'town' frock
would be worth 'anything near the marvellous crêpe-de-chine
or silk dressing-gown, in old rose, cerise, or Tiepolo pink'; or
when Albertine dons a magnificent Fortuny gown, the sleeves
of which are 'lined in cerise pink, a colour so particular to
Venetians that it is called Tiepolo pink'. And, with a small
chromatic variation, there is a further instance when Oriane
de Guermantes is wearing an evening coat in 'a magnificent
Tiepolo red'. In fact Giambattista Tiepolo loved pink, he
adored all the pinks, from the most pastel of shades to the
most dazzling, from the palest to the brightest (from whence
'cerise pink', that almost oxymoronic colour mentioned by
Proust). The gentle satiny pink of naked female flesh, alluring
legs tumbling towards you from the ceilings and the darker
pinks of firmly erect breasts, and darker still the clothes. And,
especially, the nacreous, brilliant pinks of the clouds which
set out to invade the blue of the heavens, the whole sky
turning into a sensuous rose colour. As if, in the end, the
whole firmament were a gigantic, blushing skin. The painter
of ceilings, wrote Robin in the eighteenth century, 'must
enlarge the spaces by multiplying the planes, and producing
an ensemble of the most pleasant movement and shapes. This
genre of painting is a crown added to all the embellishments
of the art of building; or, to be identified with it even more,
like a shining skin that through its lustre gives life to the most

ordered forms of beauty.' This must be taken literally in Giambattista Tiepolo's case. Through colour, he incarnates his ceilings, gives them substance. His painting is a dermatological operation, re-covering the ceilings of the great formal rooms in the palazzi with a soft desirable skin. The celestial vault is like desirable, palpitating female flesh on the point of succumbing, when it suffuses with a blush, when her modesty is offended, or rather her excitement mounts. The ceilings of drawing-rooms and bedrooms must have seen some glorious women in the eighteenth century, especially on those evenings when the nobility invited well-paid beauties to their mad parties.

If pink, for many among us, is Venice's quintessential colour, it is because it is the colour of pleasurably excited flesh. And we all recall Jean-Jacques Rousseau's Zulietta, receiving him in a more than flirtatious state of disabille, adorned in the fashion of Venice with 'her sleeves and neckline...edged with a silk thread decorated with pink pompons, that enlivened her beautiful skin' (*Confessions*). Here the pleasure is contagious, spreading everywhere with the speed of a powder trail, exciting even the sacred. Take the very carnal *Holy Family* where Veronese squeezes into 'the tight space of the frame sulphur pinks, rose pinks, mauve pinks – all the pinks his genius can muster' (André Fraigneau, *Les Enfants de Venise*). The warmth and opulence of the flesh tones and fabrics exalt holiness itself. And how, in La Serenissima, can the very stone of the buildings remain cold and insensitive to the irresistible mounting of pleasure? If, when you look at Venetian architecture what is most frequently noticeable is the presence of white of Istrian marble, and the red of brick, you are paying too little attention to Verona marble, and this is most probably because its colours have faded somewhat with time. Generally one can only distinguish the veins of a very pale, very attenuated salmon pink. 'One can just trace the colour; for Verona [marble] in long ages tends to lose its calcium or

lime, leaving the clay' (Adrian Stokes, *The Quattro Cento*).
But if you look very carefully, in many places, you can still
see it, on the edge of the steps of numerous bridges, on the
walls of the Doge's palace, on the floor of the Frari and of San
Zanipolo where it alternates with Istrian marble in a
diamanté motif, brightening these buildings with a rich
light, on the lower panels of the outside walls of Santa Maria
di Miracoli, where the bars of Verona marble are laid out in
the form of a cross. In all these places, the architecture, with
its light veining of pink, begins to take on immodest flesh
tones, like the milky-complexioned faces of women, where
pleasure has, imperceptibly, made their veins stand out. It is
as though, in Venice, the very petrification of marble cannot
escape the immodest colours of aroused flesh. 'How can one
express these pink tones of the ducal palace, that appear like
living flesh?' Théophile Gautier wonders in *Italia*. André
Suarès goes one better in *Le Voyage du Condottiere* and calls
it 'One of the most beautiful surfaces in the world, and so
alive in its enormous, pink, flesh-like nudity'.

In any case, who has not seen the white marble of La
Serenissima turn pink with the setting sun? The
unforgettable spectacle of St Mark's, so pale all day long in
summer, changing to pink at the end of the afternoon. And
now all the architecture becomes organic, living flesh,
incarnated and irrigated by the light which subtly varies its
tints. 'The golden blood of light,' Suarès writes, 'that, as
usual, cannot refrain from overdoing it, streams across the
façades, in a nuptial effusion.'

∽ Brick red ∾

In 'Venice the red / Not a boat that moves, / Not a fisherman on the water, / Not a lantern,' wrote Alfred de Musset in his *Contes d'Espagne et d'Italie*. Yes, Venice is quite red, almost as red in certain districts as Siena, which is saying something. Visually, the red of the brick preserves the burning memory of its firing in the kilns, reminding us of hot summer days, as if from summer to summer the town had ripened. This red is the colour of much of the rough cast, but also and more so the colour of the bricks that are visible when the rough cast flakes off in sheets. Now the buildings' flesh is exposed to the quick, and these great red patches, the vividness of which is constantly refreshed and revived by erosion, are like blood oozing from the palazzi and the churches. So what then is Venetian red? 'It is not a bright colour. The material used to paint the façades contains brick dust. This Venetian red is a solid, robust colour' (Pier Maria Pasinetti, *Piccolo veneziane complicate*). Red is the colour of the power of Venice, which strove to impose enduring authority over the seas. For me, the most beautiful brick reds can be found in the great buildings of the Arsenale, the rope factories, the sailmakers', the warehouses, slipways, such as those that Joseph Mallord William Turner painted, transforming them into a flamboyant, incandescent watercolour (*The Arsenal*, London, Tate Britain). The fiery reds of the crenellated walls, all the more massive and impressive because the artist chose a viewpoint almost at ground level, give you the impression of plunging into a burning furnace.

❧ Reds of power ❧

Every time in the past when I had a chance to visit the
Museo Correr on the Procuraties, there is one showcase that
fascinated me more than all the others and held me there for
a long time.* It was the impressive ceremonial garment of a
doge, from the eighteenth century; it was large, absolutely
plain, in a monochrome bright vermillion red. So plain that
one wonders if it had not been dyed in the blood of the
executions that he had ordered, or even in his own blood, for
so many doges were in fact put to death by an exasperated
public and by mistrustful patricians. And it was precisely
between those two great red columns on the Piazzetta that
these capital punishments took place in La Serenissima.

Always there were these superb red garments for the
senators, procurators, patricians, all La Serenissima's great
dignitaries. All these reds captivate me so much more as a
man of the North, where I am used to the severe, austere black
woollen cloth with a white lace collar of the great Dutch
burgermeisters of the seventeenth century, the drapers'
syndics, governors of the leper asylum in Amsterdam, or
regents of the old men's hospice at Haarlem, such as those
painted by Rembrandt, Ferdinand Bol and Frans Hals. In
Venice power is dressed in red. At Santa Maria Gloriosa dei
Frari, there is the sumptuous red brocade simar of Francesco
Pesaro, kneeling piously at the Virgin's feet, and the equally
red standard bearing the arms of Pope Alexander VI in the
Pala Pesaro by Titian. And Tintoretto's *The Madonna with*

---

* Unfortunately this garment is no longer on display in Venice, it has been
put back in store in a museum.

Child and Saints Sebastian, Mark and Theodore venerated by the three Camerlenghi, also known as *Madonna of the Treasurers* (Galleria dell'Accademia) has the three donors, Michele Pisani, Lorenzo Dolfin and Marino Malipiero, followed by secretaries carrying sacks of money, all dressed in sumptuous crimson red garments edged with white fur. And Tintoretto again: *The Procurator Jacopo Soranzo* (Galleria dell'Accademia), an old man with white hair and a white beard, wearing an immense red velvet coat. The *Portrait of Gerolamo Querini* by Sebastiano Bombelli (Fondazione Querini-Stampalia) shows a man, against a dark background, dressed in a huge plain red robe, trimmed with white lace at the wrists. Over it is a long sleeveless jerkin in a richly patterned crimson red brocade. *The Provveditore Antonio Renier* (Museo Civico, Padua) by Alessandro Longhi has this representative of Venetian power in Dalmatia and Albania painted in his official vermillion red costume, with a long coat of golden yellow, an imposing white wig and the baton of command on which he is leaning. In the disturbing *Portrait of the doge Marco Cornaro* (Private Collection, Venice) by Giambattista Tiepolo, Cornaro is seated on an elevated throne, in front of a large red awning, dressed in an ample garment, the red of which is emphasised by the white fur lining; he looks at us with a somewhat wild gaze. Tiepolo again, the impressive *Portrait of the Procurator Dolfin, captain general of the sea* (Fondazione Querini-Stampalia), unless this is Giovanni Querini or an unknown procurator: his face is 'tense with cunning, ambition and pride, intelligent and dangerous' (Henri de Régnier) and is literally perched on top of the gigantic red garment, from which only one hand emerges, which is resting on a book. Everything is red: his headdress, his baton of command resting on a table covered with a reddish brown cloth, the decorative pompoms. And this procurator is made even more disturbing by Tiepolo, who does not attempt to conceal his misshapen body of a semi-hunchback. The sumptuous scarlet of his official costume does not mask his physical disgrace. As always, the most sumptuous reds denote power – and first and foremost that of the doge whose scarlet silk velvet robe is highlighted with gold, for, as one knows, 'red is the colour *par excellence*, the archetypal colour, the first of all the colours. In numerous languages the same word signifies red and coloured' (Michel Pastoureau). 'According to Jewish tradition, the name of the first human being, Adam, means "red" and "living" and in languages with a Slavonic root "red" is still the same word as for "alive and beautiful". Compared with the origin and the abstraction of white and black (light and shadows), the colour of chaos and of priestly prophecy, the red of blood and life is the most powerful exorcism against pallid death and a homage of the living to the dead person' (Manlio Brusatin).

After you have passed through the sinister corridors of the New Prisons and returned to the Ducal Palace across the Bridge of Sighs and you arrive at the Hall of the Censors and the Room of the Avogaria, a disturbing assembly of paintings awaits you. These are the grave and severe magistrates, often bearded, and all dressed in red, painted by Domenico Tintoretto and his studio, Pietro Malombra, Leandro Bassano, Tiberio Tinelli, Sebastiano Bombelli, Pietro Uberti and Vicenzo Guarana. While the purpose of the censors was to see that the laws were properly followed regarding nominations for the bodies of state, the *avogadori*, the Republic's municipal lawyers, were the public prosecutors at the meetings of the Council of Ten, charged equally with ensuring the strict observance of constitutional laws and the recovery of fines. All these reds are the reds of power dressing, but also of the blood of the condemned. But, in any case, for centuries the finest reds came from the holocaust of millions of animals, or rather animalcules, used to dye the smallest of garments, the smallest piece of fabric. Vermillion red, or vermillion, is extracted from the verminculus, a small worm used in dyeing. Venetian crimson red, that dark, almost violet red, is an extract of the *kirmiz*, cochineal from Armenia. And throughout the whole of Antiquity, millions of murex and sea snails (*Murex trunculus, Murex Brandaris, Purpura haemastoma*) were sacrificed to extract the imperial scarlet from their glands.

Every time I walk through the *calli* of Venice, and pass carabinieri, smiling and debonnaire, or when I see them passing along the canal in a greyish blue motor boat , with the red stripe down the side of their trousers, I cannot help but recall the cruel intransigence of La Serenissima's power.

∞ Glorious red ∞

20 March 1518. A huge, joyful and impatient crowd are jammed together in the central nave of Santa Maria Gloriosa dei Frari. People jostle one another for a place in the front rows. It is the Feast of St Bernard, to whom the Franciscans avow a special devotion. And so they are using this solemn ceremony to unveil the great altarpiece of *The Assumption*, which Titian has just finished for the main altar, and which until now has been concealed from the faithful. There is impatience and silence in the assembly, for the unveiling of a work of art is a very important event for them. At last, the great curtains are drawn back. The public are stunned, overwhelmed by the grandiose composition, disconcerted, disorientated, sometimes (rarely) carried away, moved. The shocked, almost scandalised crowd begins to mill around. Even Father Germano, the prior of the Franciscan convent of the Frari, who had commissioned Titian to carry out the work, is rendered speechless, completely astounded by the gigantism of the apostles in this painting, which is nearly seven metres high (even though Titian had already explained to him many times, while the painting was being done, that seen from a distance, these figures would seem much smaller), and undoubtedly even more bewildered by the powerful symphony of reds that enliven and inflame it. The whole of the central pyramid piles three reds, pink, vermillion and scarlet, one on top of the other, and they in turn are overhung by the brownish red of God the Father.

136

If there were some people (in truth very few) who recognised in this picture the magnificent beginnings of a new pictorial style, there were many others, particularly Venetian painters, who gave this new altarpiece a poor reception and criticised it: 'And yet this was the first public work that he painted in oil,' wrote Lodovico Dolce in his *Aretin: Dialogue on painting*, 'and he did it in a very short time, and was very young. With all this merit, ignorant painters, the blind vulgar, who hitherto had seen nothing but the dead and cold pictures of Bellin[i], Gentil[e], and Vivarino, which were without motion or relief (for Giorgione had not done as yet any public work in oils, or at most nothing but half figures and portraits), said all the ill they could of this very picture. At length, Envy growing cool, and Truth by little and little opening their eyes, the people began to wonder at the new manner found out at Venice by Titian and all the painters at that time studied to imitate him; but being put out of their own way found themselves at a stand.' It is true that Titian was very confident. The whole composition has this fabulous ascending movement, with the apostles raising their arms towards heaven, while the Virgin, with her rolling eyes, has an incredible, sensual and immodest ecstasy, that is comparable only to Bernini's *Ecstasy of Saint Theresa* at Santa Maria della Vittoria in Rome. There are subtle variations in the scale of reds, from a vermillion red to crimson madder lake (modern terminology obviously) present at every stage in the representation, the dark red cloak of God the Father, the immense bright red dress of the Virgin, the red tunics of many of the apostles. And these reds are made more intense by their juxtaposition to those of the church walls, built in red brick, that also have decorations in ochre brick, which are equally present in the painting. Titian was undoubtedly not the first Venetian painter to favour red. The three Vivarinis, Antonio, his brother Bartolomeo and Alvise, Antonio's son, had shown a taste for the most beautiful reds. And I have always had a weakness for the scarlet red tunic of the elegant Saint Roch of Bartolomeo at San Eufemia, on the Giudecca. At the Frari even the two triptychs by Bartolomeo Vivarini, *The Enthroned Virgin holding the Infant Jesus on her Knees* and *Saint Mark with the Angel Musicians and Saints*, show us many saints dressed in the most splendid red vestments. But with the Vivarinis the reds have only a decorative role in the long run, whereas in Titian's *Assumption* they are the dynamic structure of the composition. And, God knows, Titian would hang on to his flamboyant reds above all else. As proof, we have this letter of 1548, sent by Aretino to a courier by the name of Lorenzetto. From Augsburg, 'Messire Titian has asked me, with the most passionate insistence, and enjoins me to write to you to beg you to send him, please, without delay, and for the sake of friendship, a half pound of that Lake that is so blazing and splendid in its true scarlet colour that, beside it, the crimson of velvet and satin appears less beautiful.' When Titian wanted to glorify the subject of his painting, he always used red. Look at all those reds in the fabulous, though unfinished, *Portrait of Paul III with his Grandsons* (Naples, Museo Capodimonte). Everything takes place in front of a splendid red curtain, which has been artfully pinned back. In the centre, seated on a red chair and with one hand resting on a table covered with a red cloth, the sovereign pontiff, an old man with a beard, then aged seventy-seven, wears a cape and cap in crimson red. Behind him to his left stands Alessandro Farnese, vice-chancellor in a red cassock and beretta, whom his grandfather had nominated a cardinal at the age of fourteen. On his right, his grandson Ottaviano, son-in-law of Charles V, in a black and red jacket, who would later rebel (with his brother's secret approbation) against the old pope, at the time of an international litigation about a part of territory belonging to his father Pier Luigi Farnese, assassinated in 1547. This family painting, begun the preceding year, was therefore never finished, and all that remains is this glorious symphony of reds which invade and light up the whole canvas. But the most glorious of all Titian's reds is without any doubt that of the huge royal coat that his friend Aretino wears (Florence, Palazzo Pitti, Galleria Palatina). Visibly overflowing with booming vitality, Aretino, an enormous, bearded *bon viveur*, holds an edge of his coat in one hand by its enormous collar. One cannot imagine a more splendid outfit than this red silk velvet which is fired with shimmering ripples of golden yellow.

∞ Blood red ∞

On 5 August 1571, Captain Marcantonio Bragadin, who commanded the Venetian garrison at Famagusta on Cyprus proposed to Lala Mustafa Pasha, commander of the Turkish land forces, that he come for the official hand-over of the keys of the city to him. Since 1 August the white flag had been flying over the ramparts. Under siege since 17 September of the preceding year, the Venetian defenders, reduced to 500 men and lacking victuals and ammunition, had decided to surrender, to avoid the massacre and pillage that would ensue, according to the tacit rules of war. Having accepted the astonishingly generous terms of peace, the Turks authorised all the Italians to embark for Crete, and the Greeks either to stay in Cyprus with some reliable guarantees, or to go into exile with a safe-conduct to the country of their choice. But, after welcoming Bragadin and his escort with the greatest courtesy, Mustafa became increasingly edgy and finally flew into a violent rage. Suddenly drawing a knife, he sliced off the Venetian commander's ear, and ordered one of his officers to cut off his other one along with Bragadin's nose. This was the beginning of the massacre, and 350 heads of the victims of the slaughter were piled up outside Mustafa's tent. 'But the worst fate had been reserved for Marcantonio Bragadin. He was held in prison for nearly a fortnight by which time his untreated wounds were festering and he was already seriously ill. First he was dragged round the walls with sacks of earth and stones on his back; next tied into a chair, he was hoisted to the yardarm on the Turkish flagship and exposed to the taunts of the sailors. Finally he was taken to the place of execution, in the main square, tied naked to a column, and, literally, flayed alive. Even this torture he is said to have borne in silence for half an hour, until, as the executioner reached his waist, he finally expired. After the grim task was completed, his head was cut off, his body quartered, and his skin, stuffed with straw and cotton, and mounted on a cow, was paraded through the streets' (John Julius Norwich, *History of Venice*).

In the sixteenth century it was not good to be a Venetian falling into the hands of the Turks, and anyone who gets carried away by airy aestheticism at the sight of Venice, ought to remember events like this. Mustafa proudly offered Marcantonio Bragadin's skin to the sultan, but nine years later, one of the rare survivors of the siege of Famagusta, Girolamo Polidoro, managed to steal it from the Arsenal at Constantinople and bring it back to Venice, where he gave it to Bragadin's sons. They laid it to rest in the church of San Gregorio. On 18 May 1596, this glorious relic was transferred to Santi Giovanni e Paolo and placed in a niche, behind the urn that forms part of the hero's memorial. It is still there, as was confirmed in 1961 when the monument was being restored and they discovered a lead coffer in which they found several pieces of tanned human skin. These were returned to the same place when the restoration work was finished.

When Titian painted *The Torture of Marysas* (Kromenz, Statnamek) in the 1570s, he could not have helped but remember Marcantonio Bragadin's frightful end at Famagusta. We know that in the myth the Phrygian satyr Marysas was burned alive by Apollo, who had won a musical competition in which he was challenged by the satyr, the one playing the flute, the other the lyre. According to the pact that they had concluded between them, the winner could inflict the punishment of his choice on the loser. Seated on the right, we can see King Midas who judged the competition: he is wearing donkey's ears as a sign of the punishment inflicted by Apollo whom he had not recognised as the victor in the musical competition with Pan. On the left, the young man holding a lyre is undoubtedly Apollo (or perhaps Olympus, a pupil of Marysas). In the centre of the composition, and crowned with the victor's laurels, is Apollo, who is helping two satyrs to set fire to the all too proud Marysas. Armed with small cutlasses they are conscientiously removing the skin of the unfortunate Marysas who is strung up by his hooves. The whole painting, which shows unbearable anatomical cruelty and is literally dripping with the victim's blood, is treated in greens and reds that are almost rust coloured.

In its very barbarism, *The Torture of Marysas* serves both as an illustration of the courage of the Venetian officers and as an allegory of painting such as Titian practised. According to Marco Boschini, who based his account on a first-hand one by the painter Palma the Younger, if Titian, once he had established the basis of his painting 'found some thing which did not agree with his intentions, he removed some tumour of flesh, like a surgeon treating a patient, and replaced an arm whose movement was dislocated or adjusted a deformed foot, without the least pity for the victim. In operating and remodelling his characters in this way, he brought them to the highest degree of perfection...And he progressively covered those bare bones with living flesh, going over them repeatedly until all they lacked was breath itself...For the final touches, he would blend the transitions from highlights to halftones with his fingers, mixing one tint with another, or with the smear of a finger he applied a dark accent on some hidden corner to strengthen it, or with a dot of red, like a drop of blood, he would enliven some surface, in this way bringing his animated figures to completion.' Finishing a painting meant 'blooding' it. Titian put painting to fire and blood. 'They say that the saline liquid which is our blood is nothing less than the internal survival of a primitive element of the sea', Marcel Proust wrote in *Sodom and Gomorrah*. I like to think that this sanguinity of Titian's is a reverberation of the Lagoon and of the Adriatic in his paintings. The salt of the incarnate. For Venice is a living organism whose *canali* and *rii*, arteries and veins, form a network of blood vessels that beat to the rhythm of the tides.

⌀ Glowing reds ⌀

Shock. Consternation. During the night of 29 February 1996, La Fenice theatre was totally wiped out by a gigantic fire. The following summer when I wandered around the high, blackened walls, my soul in torment, the whole desolate neighbourhood was still redolent with a vile smell of burning. And without a doubt all Venetians were profoundly shocked by such destruction, which deprived them of an important part of their artistic patrimony, and even more traumatised when they believed at first that it was a criminal act intended to unseat the mayor of Venice, the philosopher Massimo Cacciari. Only later did they learn – and this was even more dizzyingly stupid – that two workmen had set fire to the theatre in order to conceal the enormous delay in the building work they had undertaken. This was a heartfelt loss since La Fenice was one of the most prestigious Venetian buildings, even though the theatre finished in 1792 from Gian Antonio Selva's plans had already burnt down in 1836 and had been reconstructed by Giambattista and Tommaso Meduna, with a neo-rococo decoration of the auditorium by Tranquillo Orsi. This was no hindrance to advertising an appeal in St Mark's Square, asking for a public subscription so that La Fenice could be rebuilt 'identically' and without any delay (most unItalian), along with an exhibition, by Interpress Photo, of many photographs of the enormous conflagration, that made one think of some pagan celebration of fire. A gigantic and disturbing red glow in the night. Bright yellows, intense oranges, and above all, fiery, incandescent reds: the flames

144

rose above the town, way up in the sky. Similar blazes of colour fascinate the Venetians. This was an inferno that was impossible to abate in the heart of a sea town, where water is everywhere. It was the height of derision and misfortune, the neighbouring *rii* had been dried out so that they could be cleaned, and the firemen had no water. Although dramatic and regrettable in its consequences, the spectacular firing of La Fenice did not simply upset the Venetians. I would certainly not have the indecency to claim that it was a cause for enthusiasm and enjoyment, that would be absurd and scandalous, but it did captivate them at least – a source of fire surging between the canals, a fire almost lying on the water in an impossible conjunction of opposites. As far back as the eighteenth century Francesco and Giacomo Guardi had seized the opportunity to paint an enormous fire that had devoured a whole area of Venice. On 28 November 1789, the fire, which had accidentally broken out in a oil shop, ravaged the *contrada* of San Marcuola, obliterating the Colombina and the Volto Santo as well as all the space between the canal and the campiello of the Anconetta, destroying no less than sixty houses and leaving 140 families homeless. On different canvases, there was still the same mob of gaping onlookers watching the high red flames licking the ruins of the buildings that were already tumbling down and consumed. On the left was the canal with a few gondolas: there the flames were literally coming out of the water, the canals had caught fire. Silvio Pellico, locked up in a cell in the Piombi, just under the roof of the Doge's Palace, would also be fascinated by a great fire which had started in a building which housed the public ovens 'one of the finest and most terrible spectacles' that one could imagine. 'The night was very dark, and because of this one could see the great whirlwinds of flame and smoke so much better, whipped up by a furious wind. Sparks were flying everywhere like a rain of fire falling from the sky. The Lagoon nearby reflected the fire. A multitude of gondolas came and went' (*My Prisons*). There is always this fascination for fire lying on the water of the canals, that one can see again in the nineteenth century in a canvas by Luigi Querana, *The Fire at the Church of San Geremia during the defence of the Republic against the Austrians* (Venice, Museo di Risorgimento) It is as though the flames ravaging the building were surging up directly from the canals.

And it will come as no surprise that the fires of the setting sun fascinated the writers and painters of Venice just as much. 'On the way back, on the side of the setting sun, the sky is like a brazier and the ramparts of the houses, the towers and the churches blot out the burning redness with their opaque blackness. It is just like a monstrous fire, such as there was in the great upheaval of the world when an eruption of lava hollowed out the earthly vegetation. It seemed as though an unleashed furnace were on fire there, beyond our view; but within sight were volleys of sparks with the dark scarlet of still burning tree trunks, and burnt-out charcoal, that had fallen down and piled up when great forests had crumbled and snapped. Their funereal shadows stretched endlessly in the reddened water' (Hippolyte Taine, *Voyage en Italie*). If in many artists' view it is autumn that confers all its splendour on Venice, it is precisely because in this season (which also magnificently symbolises the dusk of history and of the city's splendours) the sunsets are more flamboyant than at other times. Sublime aquatic conflagrations of the setting sun which create brilliance above the buildings at anchor 'a fire of splendours, a firework display of the sun's rays; the sun goes down in a heap of topaz, rubies, amethysts that the wind blows along every minute, changing the shape of the clouds; dazzling rockets shoot between La Salute's two cupolas...But what doubles the magic of the spectacle is that it is repeated in the water. This sunset that is more magnificent than any king, has the Lagoon as a mirror; all these lights, all these rays, all these fires, all these streaming phosphorescences, on the lapping waves, in sparkles, in spangles, in prisms, in trails of flame. It glitters, it scintillates, in a perpetual teeming of light' (Théophile Gautier, *Italia*). It was Ruskin who noticed that even the trees in the public gardens in Venice often appeared a dazzling red in the light of the setting sun, as if they were ablaze. There is a multitude of watercolours by Turner, with water and architecture set luminously alight with yellows, ochres, oranges and reds. For example, *A Storm at Sunset* (Cambridge, The Syndics of the Fizwilliam Museum) directly associates the water of the Lagoon with solar fire; waves and boats burn, palaces and cupolas float. More extraordinary still, *Venice, seen from Fusina* (London, Tate Britain) makes the sunset itself the subject of the picture, no longer is it content to be in the background of a composition with people. Here the few descriptive details, the gondola in the centre, and on the right the thick grasses growing on a lemon yellow shallow, lose their strictly figurative value and blend into a chromatic enchantment that harmonises the crimson and violet of the highest clouds, the yellow of the sky, the orangy red of the mist that covers the horizon, and the bluish green of the sea.

Other artists – Félix Ziem (*Venise, le palais des Doges*, Paris, Musée du Petit Palais), Auguste Renoir (*Le Grand Canal*, Boston, Museum of Fine Arts), James Whistler, (*La Salute: Sunset*, Glasgow, Hunterian Art Gallery) Claude Monet (*San Giorgio Maggiore: Sunset*, Cardiff, National Museum of Wales) – react in similar vein, multiplying and saturating the yellows and oranges of dusk. Gabriele D'Annunzio does so too, by calling the most Venetian of all his novels, *Il fuoco – The Flame of Life:* the symbol of the city 'could not be other than "an inextinguishable flame across a veil of water"'.

Always there is the same imaginary world of burning water, of the Lagoon on fire. The galleys of La Serenissima painted red, boldly sailing on the blue waves of the Mediterranean. The guns of the fighting ships. Greek fire turning the enemy vessels into torches. If the Venetians demolished the Turks so severely at Lepanto on 7 October 1571, it was especially due to the construction of a new type of ship, six tall and heavy galliasses (which were in fact *galeons di mercancia*, too large to be commercially exploited and which had been converted), prefigurations of our modern battleships, powerfully armed with cannons (from fifty to seventy) on the forecastle. Monsters almost impossible to manoeuvre by sail, but spitting fire, bullets and shells in all directions. Fire on the water: La Serenissima's maritime supremacy.

At nighttime when I watch the long torch that burns and reddens in the sky above the refineries at Marghera at the end of the Lagoon, instead of cursing modern life and its ravages, I prefer to see in it a perpetually renewed symbol of the unnatural association of fire and water.

⊘ Ginger toms ⊘

If it is true that at first sight Venice's huge population of cats seems to be mostly ginger, it is most certainly true that in the writings of many authors who feel they must mention them they almost always are. Even though in reality Venetian street cats, gutter cats, or rather *gatte di laguna* are rarely a single colour. Often tabby, ginger or brownish black (distant descendants of the Syrian tabby cat, *surián* in Venetian, they arrived from the East on merchant galleys where they were employed on board as rat catchers, under the authority of a master), often also bicoloured, a capricious mixture of white and ginger fur, when they are not tricoloured, black, white and ginger. Cats of one pure colour are seen more rarely in Venice, where totally white or totally black toms make a notable exception. But you can easily imagine why they should be ginger. They are in fact urbanised, miniaturised and domesticated second cousins of the lion of Venice, the official emblem of La Serenissima, for in 848 two bold merchants, Rustico from Torcello and Buono Tribuno from Malamocco, stole the mummified corpse of St Mark from Alexandria in Egypt, hiding it under a load of pork to prevent the Muslims from seeing it, and brought it back to the Lagoon. The winged lion of the Evangelist became the symbol of La Serenissima. Since then lions have invaded the town, and are everywhere, at the entrance to official buildings and private houses, on the top of columns, on fountains and the *margella* of wells, the arches of bridges and the pediments and frontispieces of palazzi, on their dados, their corbels and their gables, the cornices of balconies, bronze doorknockers and handles. Most often the lion is standing, its mane proudly erect, its paws well shaped, wings outstretched, holding an open book on which is engraved the words the angel addressed to Saint Mark when he made a stop on one of the islands of the Lagoon: 'Pax tibi, Marce evangelista meus' (Peace be with you, My evangelist Mark).When the book is closed, it is because the lion, so they say, was sculpted to symbolise peace.

The old stone lions of Venice have aged badly, it must be said. Over the course of the years and the centuries, they have lost much of their arrogance. The marble is pitted, crumbling, crazed, sometimes even broken. The saline air of the Lagoon has eroded the shape of their mouth, flattened the muzzle, worn away the flanks and eaten the paws. I know of one particularly lamentable one on Murano, perched high on a square pilaster near Ponte de Mezo. It has lost its wings which have broken off. Its paws are broken, and the cracks have been clumsily filled with cement. Its mouth is split, its muzzle worn, coated with black. The book which it holds with an eroded paw is crackled. It is a miracle that it has not fallen into a thousand pieces, and deplorable and saddening – it looks like an old bulldog and instils more pity than fear. Some of the lions which guard the entrance to the Arsenale, in particular one of them which was brought back from Athens in 1687 after the reconquest of Morea, are scarcely any better: they are truly sick, with cracks everywhere and broken mouths. With their heads of white stone besmirched with black, all these lions of Venice look strangely like sparrows that have been up a chimney. As a consequence of suffering the injuries of time, they have adopted a good-natured, resigned air. No longer do they roar: instead they wait for the sun to warm their old bones. The two antique raw-boned lions, in marble, on guard on either side of the door of the palazzo Marcello di Leonii, along the Grand Canal, no longer impress anyone, for they are so tired and worn. Just like the ones which watch over the entrance to the palazzo Venier dei Leoni, which got its name from the lions kept in a cage in the beautiful garden inside. All the lions of the

Grand Canal look rather alarmed when confronted with the extent of traffic on the water, and one cannot help wondering if it is they who are afraid. Not to mention the two unfortunate lions in red marble on the piazzetta dei Leoncini, to the left of St Mark's Basilica: they are not all that old, since they were sculpted in 1722, but are well worn, having served as familiar mounts for numerous generations of Venetians and visitors who attire them in masks and tricorn hats at Carnival time. Since time immemorial, the facetious and scornful Venetians have made fun of the lion surmounting the column of the piazzetta Vigo on Chioggia, by calling it the Chioggia Cat, because it is no bigger than a common tom, and, so it is said, leaving the wrapping from a packet of ham underneath it. But now their stone lions have scarcely any proud allure left. The bronze lions appear to have resisted better, nonetheless through being polished by generation after generation by the anonymous hands of passers-by, they have acquired a gentleness which is hardly compatible with their status of fearsome wild beasts.

Only the cats of Venice have retained the felinity of the lion. They alone, especially when they are ginger, remind us of Vittore Carpaccio's great lion, which decorated one of the buildings of the palazzo of the Camerlenghi at the Rialto before being transferred to the Doge's Palace. With its front paws resting on terra firma and its back ones on water to denote the two geographical milieux over which the city exerted its power, this archaic Gothic lion, with its human rather than animal teeth, is much more disturbing in its anthropomorphic state. The whole picture is painted in tawny colours as if the fur of the carnivore is reflected in the whole of the landscape and La Serenissima seen in the background.

When the first chill arrives on the Lagoon at the end of autumn, the Venetians take out their beautiful furs from their wardrobes to wear on their Sunday stroll along the Zattere. It is on the banks of the Dorsoduro, along the Giudecca canal, that Venetian families usually walk on a Sunday, in order to avoid the tourists who continue to cram into St Mark's Square and around the Rialto. Venice is still, more than ever, provincial, in spite of the city's apparent cosmopolitanism, and so, once a week, the young women and ladies like to show off their luxurious and expensive coats. All the furs, from light russet to dark brown, are brought out. Every Sunday, the she-cats walk in one direction, then in the other, along the Zattere quay.

⌾ Glass ⌾

When you are writing an essay on the aesthetics of Venice, it is considered good taste to make snide remarks at some time or another about the glassworks on Murano, or, to be more precise, about the profusion of artefacts in gaudy glass on display in the hundreds of souvenir shops that invade and disfigure all the streets in La Serenissima like a monstrous spreading cancer, pitilessly driving out all other types of shop; stupid tourists looking for tacky knick-knacks, and poor Venice debased and corrupted. And it is true that ninety-nine per cent of this cheap glassware repetitively on display from one shop window to the next are despairingly ugly and in bad taste: with groups of clowns, little orchestras of black musicians, families of animals in different sizes, scalloped fish and intertwined doves, pretty-pretty little flowers in all manner of shapes and styles, gondolas, gondoliers and sirens of every colour, fantasy jewels, bracelets and earrings in garish colours, bottles, fruit dishes, ash trays, chandeliers. A whole crystalline flora and fauna for nests of dust (and always sold under the Venetian label, but often manufactured in Hong-Kong or Taiwan) which will end up on the mantelpiece in lower middle-class households the world over. The Murano glassworks can in fact achieve an hallucinating and unbelievable degree of hideousness. In the summer of 1997, for example, insects were all the rage and I was horrified by all the scarabs and cockroaches, and spiders in their webs. Luckily glass is by nature fragile. But isn't all this to do with a secular tradition? Ever since the sixteenth century Murano has mass-produced cheap-looking trinkets on an industrial scale – *millefiore,* pearl mosaics, *margherite,* little pearls ('for knitting and embroidery'), the *veriselli* – small coloured fragments that are perfect imitations of precious stones. And Marco Polo brought back from China a whole cargo load of these false gems set in gold mounts, rocaille, rounded pearls which took on the appearance of carved Charlottes when they are facetted irregularly, so many sorts of 'Venetian pearls' which are worth more for their exuberant colours than for the originality of their shapes. This was a flourishing industry from the time of the Renaissance, for these pearls were generally used as barter with the indigenous tribes in the colonies. And when Chateaubriand saw an artisan spin a fine rope of glass on Murano, 'it was of this glass, ' he recalled with melancholy, 'that the pearl was made, which hung from the nose of the little Iroquois girl at Niagara Falls: a Venetian hand had crafted a savage's fal-de-lal' (*Mémoires d'outre-tombe*). At the end of the nineteenth century, Murano began to produce pearls streaked with bright colours, cynically called 'African' because they were used as bartered merchandise in Africa. Venice has been commercial and venal since time immemorial, it has always sold knick-knacks and souvenirs. As long ago as 1291, in a move to avoid disastrous fires which regularly ravaged La Serenissima's wooden buildings, the authorities passed a law that obliged glassmakers to install their furnaces on Murano. It was then that an era of immense prosperity began: azure glass, mirrors and lights from Murano dazzled and seduced all the European sovereigns from the Escurial to Potsdam. The master glassblowers were forbidden, on pain of banishment for life, or even death, to export the ancient secrets of their industry by working outside Venice, which had learned how to be protectionist to assure its wealth. All this brilliant glassware was exchanged for tea and silk with the Chinese who made buttons from it for the mandarins' garments, and exchanged for furs with the American Indians, for palm oil, gold dust and slaves with the Africans. After all, a beautiful slave in good health, in the eighteenth century, was worth just four pounds of pearls.

And I have to admit that for a long time, too, I myself have scorned Murano and its knick-knacks, advising all my relations and friends against this abominably 'touristy' excursion. The setting-down point on Murano is harsh, almost depressing, with its heavy barges loaded down with bales of straw and packing cases, its factories with their faded commercial signs and towering black chimney stacks, its great warehouses where the merchandise is stocked. 'It is a sinister place,' Aragon said, who as an aesthete of the first order mistrusted places where the very people whom he defended politically worked. 'This island of glassmakers from which come those blown and gilded artefacts, wild pearls, extraordinary flowers, lights and mirrors, candy sugar candlesticks and dreamy boiled sweets, can hardly be called a town and is surrounded by factories, although at the church of San Pietro Martire, there is a Madonna by Bellini that dates back to the end of the fifteenth century, a Christian Venus amidst this sea spray of glass. Nothing is more dilapidated, more miserable, more rundown than Murano. To the piteous state of its walls can be added the human misery, the degradation of the work, widespread consumption, child deaths, anaemia of a race worn out by glass blowing' (*Les Voyageurs de l'Impériale*). It was fifty years ago that Aragon wrote these lines, but even now in spite of all the municipality's efforts to restore Murano's historic centre, the island, a dismal working-class suburb of Venice, still remains rather sad, like all other industrial sites. The few palazzi that survive on the edge of the canal look slightly lost among the rundown walls of the factories. No matter that they bear the names of famous Venetian families such as Da Mula, Gustinian and Corner, their fame is extinguished irreparably. Long gone are Murano's splendid gardens, decked with vines and fruit trees, that were once thought of as real earthly paradises: Andrea Navagero cultivated the rarest botanical species here, and literary academies held meetings, entertaining the most prestigious of guests with floral games and poetic jousts: guests such as Aretino, Petro Bembo, Tasso, Sansovino. Long gone, too, the luxurious *casini* belonging to the rich nobility of Venice, where they connived to lure beautiful young nuns, dying of boredom in the numerous convents nearby. Casanova himself had an ardent adventure here with a certain M.-M., a delightful nun from the convent of San Giacomo di Galizzia. On their first night together, Giacomo gave her seven solid hours of the most positive proofs of his ardour, and of the feelings she inspired in him. As it was, the licentiousness prevailing in Murano became proverbial. And seventeen churches on the island were barely enough to cope with the confessions of all the sins taking place on the island. When the libertines had grown tired of their love games, they went to play at the Mocenigo casino, the ceilings of which had been painted by pupils of Veronese with dizzying trompe-l'oeil. All that has well and truly vanished. Murano is no longer a place of delight, a haven of pleasure.

Yet Venice would not be Venice without Murano, for there is nothing more consubstantial with the very nature of La Serenissima than the secular art of its master glassmakers. First because of their very technique which consists of working with water and fire. Enter without the slightest qualm, like the most ordinary tourist, into one of those ateliers along the rio dei Vetrai, preferably choosing a serious factory (some still exist on Murano), like Venini, SIV, Salviati, Moretti. Immediately the heat from the furnace hits you in the face. Admire the spectacular dexterity with which the glassmakers manipulate and turn those hollow metal rods with the small lumps of incandescent glass on the end. Admire the virtuosity of those inexhaustible glassblowers who, at will, can produce a bottle, a vase or an animal. Inflating, distending, drawing out with their breath and bending, twisting, cutting, goffering with their pincers, the glowing red molten agglutination. When it comes to elaborating a more refined piece, the number of manipulations must be multiplied: blowing, extinguishing at the right moment, dousing, watching the temperatures and the baths. A constant alternation between fire and water. If Venice is duty-bound to produce glass, it is, from the evidence, a transposition and a materialisation of water. Towards the middle of the fifteenth century, Angelo Barovier invented a special glass which took the name of 'cristallo', because it was so pure, as transparent and as clear as rock crystal. And from then on glass made possible the unimaginable: the hardening of water, the petrification of the fleeing, ungraspable wave, the mineralisation of the Lagoon. 'If in fantasy, the stones of Venice appear as the waves' petrification, then Venetian glass, composed of Venetian sand and water, expresses the taut curvature of the cold under-sea, the slow, oppressed yet brittle curves of dimly translucent water' (Adrian Stokes, *The Stones of Rimini*). In other words, solidified water and along with it all the fishes it shelters, like the ones Henri de Regnier invented, when he bought a huge supply of glassware on Murano; so that he and his friends could set about decorating it with a brush: 'There were baskets full of miniature flasks like the fry of miraculous fish. All this glass looked as though it had been retrieved from the bottom of the Lagoon with a gigantic fishing net. It had a cold, fishy appearance and it lingered at the end of one's fingers like a smell of the sea' (*L'Altana ou la Vie vénetienne*). Glass is intimately Venetian, too, because it makes all the chromatic metamorphoses completely possible. Not only because the metallic oxides provide a marvellous scale of colours: copper, according to the quantity used gives green, turquoise, blue, red; iron, bluey green and yellow; cobalt, dark blue and light blue; manganese, violet purple and brown; silver, strong beige; gold, pink and red; the mixture of tin and silver, opal; the mixture of cobalt and iron, blue green, that of manganese and chrome, black. But also because all the colours can be either transparent, translucent or opaque. They can have the brightness of precious stones, the dense opacity of certain minerals, or even look like porcelain.

In the nineteenth century, the great tradition of Venetian glass sank more and more into the worst commercial mediocrity, in spite of efforts made in the 1880s by a new generation of master glassblowers, among them Vincenzo Moretti. He was the first to produce *murrini*, a technique that imitates Byzantine and Roman mosaics. First small pastilles of coloured glass are produced by cutting specially made sticks of glass, and then a collection of these fused *tesserae* are applied while still hot, in a regular pattern. For a real renaissance to occur on Murano, one would have to wait till the twentieth century and the 1920s, when Paolo Venini founded an enterprise in which he tried to continue using traditional methods and designs without cutting himself off from modern creations, and recruited Carlo Scarpa who abandoned any vague, purely decorative scheme. What mattered first and foremost for him was that the decoration, which until then had not been a truly integral part of the whole should come directly and uniquely from the material itself. 'Material and decoration are a single entity, made together, blended together from the original lump of glass. Blown glass should never look like porcelain which has been painted. Light is imprisoned inside the glass and always gives it depth. Even when glass is at its most opaque. Its colours, its design, its inclusions arise from within it. That is why Scarpa's glass has a particularly lively, organic look' (Elisabeth Vedrenne, *Scarpa-Venini*). The inner luminosity of glassware was combined with the great Venetian pictorial tradition. It would have the most astonishing and the most truly Venetian results when he tried embellishing the complex technique of *sommersi* which produced 'a very thick glass, made of different superimposed layers. A sort of translucid lamination of changing colours.' The glass had to be plunged several times into more molten glass in order to apply hot, gold or silver leaf each time, which would then spread into tiny bubbles. 'It was as though the object containing tiny bubbles and filigree,' Carlo Scarpa wrote magnificently, 'had been plunged into water and, when being withdrawn, a part of this water had remained clinging to the surface without losing any of its transparency. How many effects were now possible! How many little bubbles of air glinted like small gold sequins through the brilliance of the submerged surface. What depth the veins, the folds, the repeated layers took on...' Nothing is more extraordinary than all those aqueous nuggets created by Scarpa, that have deep fluid transparencies, as though heavy and muddy. Here one comes closest to the waters of the Lagoon and their reflections. 'Dark, moiréed water, with an oily patchiness made by sun or storm. Some of Scarpa's tones – greens, bronzes, the colour of brine, of sand, amber, neither greens nor blues, metallic tones, mauve, glaucous tints – evoke the real Venice better than his magnificent poppy reds or sun yellows that in turn evoke Burano's walls' (Elisabeth Vedrenne). One day I saw a vase in green *corroso* glass, about thirty centimetres high, that looked exactly like a solidified chunk of Lagoon water. It was a deep mysterious watery green, between cobalt green and cadmium green, and had light iridescences, with effects like waves produced by its irregular reliefs, like marine labia. An organic water like the soft flesh of a jellyfish left on the sandy beach by the outgoing tide...

∞ Vegetal green ∞

After a bad night's sleep on the T2, you at last emerge from
Santa Lucia station into the morning and, right ahead, you see
the Grand Canal, but what you notice immediately is San
Simeone Piccolo's large, slightly grotesque cupola, shaped
like a suppository, verdigris in colour, due to the oxidisation
of the copper plates that cover it. Green, too, is the lantern
beneath a statue of Christ the Redeemer. While Napoleon
caused huge destruction elsewhere in Venice with his
unforgivable pillaging, he was right when he said: 'I have seen
churches without cupolas, but never cupolas without
churches', for the façade, which is already shortened by a
flight of steps, is crushed by the cupola's size. Here this
enormous green hulk ('like a clock tower in Oslo or
Stockholm' Sartre noted) has something indecent and
incongruous about it and, in real terms the green is somewhat
unseemly and out of place in Venice. Dare I say that the horses
at St Mark's make the same bad impression on me, especially
since the originals have been carefully removed to a safe place
and have been replaced by copies? For if those quadrupeds
that were stolen from Constantinople still retained some
(modest) traces of gilding, this new quadriga is of a plain,
aggressive green bronze, that the restorers would have done
well to gild with leaf. As has been done, for example, with the
enormous globe upheld by two solid bronze kneeling figures
of Atlantes at the Dogana di Mare, at the extreme end of the
Giudecca.

Every time I go up or down the Grand Canal, I still feel
astonished by those little gardens, with a few palms,

magnolias and orange trees which are set out in front of some of the palazzi. While I cannot ignore that Venice has many gardens, that Henri de Régnier celebrated in his *Esquisses vénetiennes,* here the vegetation always surprises me, disturbs me even. In Venice I can never help myself associating the green of nature with the heartrending spectacle of Torcello. All the wild, profuse, odiferous vegetation that now occupies the island has taken the place of the Venice before Venice, which is slowly dying before disappearing almost completely. Willows and poplars, bushes and weeds grow freely where once palazzi and churches stood: the vegetal has gained ascendancy over the mineral. And, even in Venice, I always have the unpleasant feeling that, if the gardens are often enclosed behind red walls, it is less because of lack of space than as a means of preventing them from spreading and eating up the town.

There are, however, certain gardens, particularly on the Giudecca, that I have loved for a brief while, the time length of a walk, when Venice is overwhelmed by the heat and their coolness refreshed me. But, in the final instance, it's hopeless, they seem to me to be always rather out of place, because Venice owes nothing to nature, is even a town *contre nature,* to quote Chateaubriand's phrase. It is pure artifice, an incredible challenge to geographical, hydrographical, climatic conditions. Here the real forest is underground, submerged: there are these hundreds of thousands, millions of tree trunks, of oak, elm, or larch (no less than 1,100,000 piles just for La Salute alone) which consolidate the mud and support the palazzi and the churches. Every time I touch those soft green, slimy seaweeds that have risen from the bottom of the Lagoon to its surface, every time I see those green viscous plants on the slippery steps of marble staircases at the *rii*'s edge, that 'sinister green that the sea caresses and keeps alive at the base of the palazzi' (Balzac), I imagine they are the leaves of the great forests chopped down to keep La Serenissima afloat, that are rising again from the watery depths of the murky black canals. A very literary conceit, I concede, but from a strictly scientific point of view, the green seaweed threatens the very foundations of Venice. The great *Ulva rigida* is particularly formidable. It feeds on pollution, it proliferates monstrously, accumulates almost a million tons a year, and not content with being a parasite on other species, and blocking canals and channels, it consumes the oxygen and releases very destructive sulphurs.

Perhaps this is why San Simeone Piccolo's cupola always tends to disturb me when I arrive in Venice: 'This building ... although unlike any other building there, in viridescent form, in a colour most unusual for Venice, symbolizes the prevailing process. This dome confounds the heights with the depths, suggesting in clear and stationary form exalted to an apex, the long tilted lift of the swell against the stones, which subsiding, reveals the greens of seaweed and slime' (Adrian Stokes *Venice*). And so to reassure myself, I would like to repeat that Venice's true surface flora consists of marble, trefoils, finials, and Gothic rose windows.

Often, at the end of the day, I go to sit in front of La Salute, on the few white marble steps which descend into the greenish water of the Grand Canal. Depending on the water level, four or five wet steps emerge, always covered more or less with a delicate fringe of hairy seaweed that oscillates to the rhythm of the ebb and flow of the little waves, or is violently shaken at regular intervals when a vaporetto has just passed. How gentle and caressing these seaweeds at first seem with their rocking movements, but it is enough to take a careful look at the state of the steps – the rounded angles, the small cracks in the marble, the blocks that have come unstuck – to understand the infinite patience and the formidable tenacity with which these fine vegetal filaments insinuate themselves between the stones, undermining the foundations, eating away the mineral.

And if there is really one place that I always carefully

avoid while I am in Venice, it is the Giardini publici, created by Napoleon, who, in order to make way for them, had part of the marshes drained and ruthlessly razed to the ground many precious sacred buildings, among which were the church and monastery of San Domenico di Castello, the church and the convent of Sant'Antonio di Castello, as well as the Ospedale di Gesù Christo which had been a home for old sailors at the end of their lives. The Venetians themselves would never have had the idea of a vast garden like this, which is very French in its conception, like a town park.

What is the point of having a lung in the town when you can breathe the air from the Lagoon and the Adriatic everywhere in Venice! Even the Giardinetti, near the Piazzetta, find no favour in my eyes except in summer, when they provide some shade for those colonies of painters and water-colourists following the age-old Venetian tradition of selling views of La Serenissima to passing foreigners. In fact when it comes to it, rich Venetians have always had gardens, immense and splendid parks, ever since the sixteenth century, but on terra firma, all along the Brenta canal. The town is for the town and the countryside is for the countryside, each in its place. Take a long walk in the superb park at the Villa Pisani at Stra, with its semicircular portico, its belvedere, its orangery, its fountains and especially its famous labyrinth, celebrated by Gabriele d'Annunzio in *Il Fuoco*. And you can readily imagine that the Venetian patrician needed to stay for long periods on terra firma, in the countryside, in summer and autumn, in the season of the *villegiatura*, when the overheated, unhealthy town was invaded with foetid miasmas, just so that he could forget that he was living in a ship of stone that, one day, could well be swallowed up in the depths of the sea. It is no coincidence, therefore, if the greenest of all La Serenissima's painters, Lorenzo Lotto, though born of pure Venetian stock, chose a career as an independent artist and worked for a great deal of the time on terra firma, at Treviso and Rome, in the Marches and at Bergamo. He had a marked taste for large green draperies which he used as a background in his portraits. More fascinating still is a strange, murky predominance of green in certain of his compositions, for example in *The Triumph of Chastity* (Rome, Pallovicini Collection). Never would a Venetian from Venice have favoured green to this point. Never!

∽ Dark green ∾

The shutters of Venice are almost always very, very dark green, almost black, at least when they are newly painted. With the sea climate they discolour and peel very quickly. Then there are numerous large cypresses which jut out above the pink walls of San Michele, like tall candles: they too are a very dark green. Then there is the green of ivy on the crenellations of the walls of the Arsenale, like land seaweed eating away the defunct power of the city. I also remember, on the day after a terrible storm which had massacred the plantations and the trees, just in front of La Malcontenta, the water of the Brenta was then a strong green, full of vegetation, slowly bearing weeds, bits of plants, leaves and small branches torn off by the tempest towards the Lagoon. A murky green plant soup, almost thick and sticky, stuffed full and saturated with a repellent and disturbing vegetable richness.

So that's it for dark green, I can find nothing further. But what if, in fact, the whole history of Venetian painting can be summed up in one progressive passage from blues and greens still present in the artists of the fifteenth century, to a massive predominance of tawny and fiery tones, ochres, oranges and reds?

∽ Veronese green ∽

It was a character in Jean Thuillier's fine novel, *Campo morto*, a certain Teodoro who chose the famous Veronese green as a colour fetish for himself, explaining it thus: 'Why choose a green so tender, so gentle, so young and agreeable? Because this green is as deceitful, as fraudulent, as swindling as I am, I who deceive the world. This suave and delicate colour is an atrocious poison, as murderous as the Borgias' of whom it is brother. Look, Doctor, have you perhaps forgotten your chemistry? Copper arseniate is Veronese green, and toads burnt with arsenic in copper vessels were the Borgia's poison.' A pigment that intoxicates you – that would be such a fascinating colour that you might conceivably get hooked on this green like a hard drug. Look at, for example, the story of the jeweller, Luciano Venturi (in one of the short stories in Marcel Schneider's *La fin du carnaval*), so expert in his choice of precious stones, so adept at mounting them and adding value to their *éclat*: 'Luciano was totally bewitched by the colour of the stones. He loved the intense cold green of the emerald, the changing green of the chrysoprase, the autumnal green of the peridot, the pale, almost livid amazonite, the malachite with streaks of fresh lettuce. His favourite colour was Veronese green, a bizarre choice since it was an invention of the painter and could not be found in nature, but Luciano would not let a contradiction stop him. The only disturbing side to his character was just this – his love of Veronese green. He could have killed man or woman to possess a jewel of this colour. And who knows what they might have done to him afterwards – the gibbet or the galleys, would not have fazed him. At the climax of his nocturnal dreams, when he succeeded in snatching the unique stone, a monster of nature that he had pursued with frenzy, with despair, what do you think he did? He fucked it with devotion and clasped it to his bosom with a deep sigh...' Happily the climax of his dreams would not lead to crime or rape. He would find happiness the day, when disguised as an old-time Pulchinella, he was lucky enough to have a marvellous night of passion with a very pretty, masked Venetian lady, also dressed in a gown of his favourite colour, 'the most beautiful, the most pure of Veronese greens that one could dream of. Where had she found such a rare, almost unfindable fabric? She was surely a noble woman, or a dancer, or a rich foreigner... She wore a silk mask decorated with lace which fell as far as her lips and a veil, elegantly fixed in her hair.' What a marvellous thrill for Luciano Venturi to make love to Veronese Green, since this is the name that he hurries to give this beautiful woman. The climax of the whole affair is that this famous appellation, this so-called Veronese green, the subject of so many aesthetes' and writers' dreams and fantasies, has strictly speaking no connection with a specific pigment used by the Venetian master. The usage of 'Veronese green', a variety of pigments from copper and arsenic, goes back no further than the nineteenth century. Specialists who have analysed the *Marriage at Cana* during its recent restoration in fact discovered 'no rare pigment, nothing special in the composition of the greens. The same copper pigment appears to colour the whole of the green drapes in the painting. It is a neutral acetate of copper, more commonly called verdigris and called *verde eterno* by the Venetian painters. To tone down the too-blue nuance of the pure pigment, yellow is mixed with the greens. This technical procedure, familiar to all the painters of the period, was used systematically by Veronese in the light greens and the dark greens... The differing values of green are obtained by varying the concentration of yellow and by adding lead white.' What a terrible fall from grace, from Veronese green to verdigris, the green that comes from the oxidisation of copper. Even so, when the modern restorers of this immense canvas discovered under the relatively opaque and dull red cloak of the intendant 'a green material that was luminous, shaped, worked', they decided there and then to remove this overpainting, although it was very old (since it contained the characteristic materials of the Venetian palette of the seventeenth century). I have even so problems in believing that the definitive removal of the red overpainting was on the sole basis of purely scientific criteria (valuable though they are, in the absence of all historical documentation). With Veronese, green should prevail over red. The name 'Veronese green' is pure fiction, but in reality there is nothing more influential than fiction. At least there is still a chance.

❧ Purple ❧

There is certainly no colour more saturated than purple which is a crimson gone wrong, and none so artificial, either, since in nature purple colours are relatively rare. I am not surprised that in Veronese's *Judith and Holophernes* (Caen, Musée des Beaux-Arts), which originally decorated the palazzo Bonaldi in Venice, the large skirt of the black serving maid who is preparing to put the dismembered head of the Assyrian general in her pouch is mauve, like the bottom of Judith's dress. Not just because such a mauve goes sumptuously with her ebony skin, but also because this colour brings the torture to its climax, it clashes with the red of the blood spurting from the neck, and dripping from the head on to the ground, spattering the sheets and cushions. Purple is the colour of colour, it is colour driven to a state of apoplexy.

☙ Journeys in colour ❧

This evening, as on so many evenings when I stay in Venice, I am sitting on a terrace, right at the end of the Zattere quay, opposite the Giudecca. A huge barge sails past, carrying an enormous yellow lorry, with its red cabin: *BILLA oggi il tuo supermercato*. It comes to deliver to the supermarket close by. On the road it would be commonplace and anonymous, I would not pay the slightest attention to it. But here this displacement of colour on the blue grey of the Lagoon transcends triviality. This is the kinetics of colour in Venice, which never remains still. I had the luck today to see a superb liner arriving from a distance. Two beautiful tugs, the *Hippo* and the *Squalus*, thickset and powerful, in blacks and whites, guiding it. It was the *Danae* – a tall elegant white spindle, edged with a fine blue stripe, a yellow and blue funnel. It was soon followed by a ship of the Minoan Lines, the base of the hull red, the rest white, with a red funnel too. What an incessant traffic of colour.

I have only once arrived in Venice by liner. I had embarked at Split in former Yugoslavia and, on the Adriatic, I had long dreamed of La Serenissima such as she would appear to me from a boat. For a long time in advance I went and stood on the top deck. And little by little Venice drew near, I saw her colours unthread, I understood her chromatic immodesty, her way of yielding her colours in movement. Before leaving Venice in this summer of 1997 I climbed the campanile of San Giorgio Maggiore for the last time. On the water was a whole series of movements. The fairly rapid trajectories of numerous boats which traced long white furrows on the turquoise Lagoon. The twirling of small splashes of colour: clumsy vaporetti in black and light beige, taxis in brilliant, varnished woods, the fine black outlines of the gondolas, large barges in greens, reds, and blues, white yachts, the grey blue of the police launches, and majestic and slow, the great hulks of liners and cargo boats. The enormous red hulls of the Norse Irish Ferries. An imposing blue cargo boat from Istanbul. The great ochre mass of the *Egizia* from Venice, loaded down with lorries of every colour. The elegant white silhouette of the *Ionian Galaxy* of the Strintzis Lines. A fabulous maritime action painting, multiplying colours and outlines on the Lagoon canvas. A living Pollock, at each moment fading away and beginning again. This is the pictorial modernity of Venice, that, more than our past, is our present and our future.

∽ Bibliography ∾

[Where relevant, original sources and available English editions have been cited, rather than the French editions used by the author. Trans.]

Obviously, in a book of this kind, information has been drawn from a very wide variety of sources.

Novels, travel books, essays and correspondence devoted exclusively or in part to Venice and Venetian art

Louis Aragon, *Les voyageurs de l'Impériale*, Paris, Gallimard, 1947

Pietro Aretino, *Lettere (1492–1556)*, Editions Scala, 1988

Ferdinand Bac, *Le Mystère vénetien*, Paris, Bibliothèque Charpentier, Fasquelle, 1909

Honoré de Balzac, 'Lettre à la comtesse Clara Maffei', *Revue de France*, 1 December 1927

Paolo Barbaro, *Lunazione veneziane*, Turin, La Stampa, 1990

Martina Barover, *Carlo Scarpa. I vetri di Murano 1927–1947*, Venice, Il Gardo, 1991

Lucien Bély, *Belle Venise*, photographs by Jean-Paul Gisserot, Editions Jean-Paul Gisserot, 1993

Marco Boschini, *Le ricche minere della pittura veneziana*, Venice, 1674

Joseph Brodsky, *Watermark*, Hamish Hamilton, 1992

Charles de Brosses, *Lettres familières écrites d'Italie en 1739 et 1740*, published for the first time from the handwritten manuscripts, by M.R. Colomb, Paris, A. Levasseur, 1836

André Bruyère, *Sols. Saint-Marc. Venise*, Paris, Imprimerie Nationale Editions, 1990

Bibliography

Alain Buisine, 'L'oeil se perd', *Poétique*, no. 96, November 1993, Paris, Editions du Seuil

Alain Buisine, *Les Ciels de Tiepolo*, Paris, Gallimard 1996

Alain Buisine, 'Aux marges de Venise, incertitudes mouvantes', in *Venise*, Paris, Autrement, 1997

Donatella Calabi, Ugo Camerino and Ennio Concina, *La Citta degli Ebrei. Il Ghetto di Venezia, Archittetura et Urbanistica*, Venice, Albrizzi Editore, 1991

Riccardo Calimani, *Istoria del Ghetto di Venezia*, Milan, Rusconi Libri, 1985

Flavio Caroli and Stefano Zuffi, *Tiziano*. English edition, *Titian*, London, Dorling Kindersley, 1990

Chateaubriand, *Mémoires d'outre-tombe*, Paris, Gallimard, 1957

Bernard D. Cooperman and Roberta Curiel, *Il Ghetto di Venezia*, photographs by Graziano Arici, Venice, Arsenale Editrice, 1990

Gabriele D'Annunzio, *Il fuoco*, 1900. English edition, *The Flame of Life*, 1900

Gabriele D'Annunzio, *Notturno*, 1921. English edition, *Nocturne and Five Tales of Love and Death*, 1993

Anne-Marie Deschodt, *Mariano Fortuny. Un magicien de Venise*, photographs by Sacha Van Dorssen, Editions du Regard, 1979

Michael Dibdin, *Dead Lagoon*, London, Faber and Faber, 1994

Giovanni Dolcetti, *La Profumeria dei Veneziani. Cenni storici*, Venice, 1898

Lucien Fabre, *Bassesse de Venise*, Paris, Editions de la Nouvelle Revue Française, 1924

André Fraigneau, *Les Enfants de Venise*, Paris, Arléa, 1997

Carlo Fruttero & Franco Lucentini, *L'Amante senza fissa dimora*, Milan, Mondadori, 1986

Tomaso Garzoni, *La Piazza universale di tutte le professioni del mondo*, Venice, 1592

Alain Gerber, *Quatre saisons à Venise, Campo San Stefano*, Paris, Robert Laffont, 1996

Il gioco dell'amore. Le cortigiane di Venezia dal Trecento al Settecento, Milan, Berenice, 1990

Jean Giono, *Voyage en Italie*, Paris, Gallimard, 1953

Christian Giudicelli, *Quartier d'Italie*, Paris, Editions du Rocher, 1993

Goethe, *Epigrammes vénitiennes* (1790), Aubier Montigne, 1982

Edmond and Jules de Goncourt, *L'Italie d'hier – Notes de Voyages 1855–6*, Paris, G. Charpentier and E. Fasquelle, Editeurs, 1894

Edmond and Jules de Goncourt, *Notes sur l'Italie*, Paris, Editions Desjonquères/Editions de la Réunion des musées nationaux, 1996

Ernest Hemingway, *Across the River and into the Trees*, London, Jonathan Cape, 1950

Hermann Hesse, *Voyages en Italie*, Paris, José Corti, 1992

Histoire de Venise, Anthology by Sébastien Lapaque, Paris, Sortilèges, 1996

Henry James, *Italian Hours*, 1909, The Pennsylvania University Press, 1992

La Pesca in Mare. Metodi – Tecniche. Esperienze di vita, Associazione Culturale 'El Fughero', San Pietro in Volta, 1989

H.C. Robbins Landon, *Vivaldi 1678–1741*, London, Thames and Hudson, 1993

Frederic C. Lane, *Venice. A Maritime Republic*, Johns Hopkins University Press, 1973

Robert de Laroche and Jean-Michel Labat, *Chats de Venise*, Tournai, Casterman 1996

Peter Lauritzen, *Venice Preserved*, photographs by Jorge Lewinski and Mayotte Magnum, introduction by John Julius Norwich, Bethseda, U.S., Adler and Adler, 1986

D.H. Lawrence, *Lady Chatterley's Lover*, Florence 1928; full text London, Penguin, 1960

Les Venises de Tobiasse, Paris, Editions de la Différence, 1992

Bibliography

Michael Levey, *Painting in Eighteenth-Century Venice*, New Haven, Yale University Press, 1994

Jean Lorain, *Venise*, Paris, Editions de la Bibliothèque, 1997

Pierre Loti, *L'Exilée*, Paris, Calmann-Lévy, 1893

Paul Lutz, *Lions de Venise*, commentary by Marielle Médas, Editions Solar, 1997

Liliana Magrini, *Carnet vénetien*, Paris, Gallimard, 1956

Michèle Manceaux, *Pourquoi pas Venise*, Paris, Editions du Seuil, 1981

Thomas Mann, *Death in Venice* (1912) translated from the German by David Luke, London, Bantam, 1988

Charles Mauras, *Les Amants de Venise. George Sand & Musset*, Paris, E. de Boccard, 1916

Mary McCarthy, *Venice Observed*, London, William Heinemann, 1961

Agnès Michaux, *Le Roman de Venise. Un voyage à travers les plus beaux textes de la littérature*, Paris, Albin Michel, 1996

Michel de Montaigne, *Journal de Voyage en Italie par la Suisse et L'Allemagne en 1580 et 1581*, Paris, Le livre club du libraire, 1957

Paul Morand, *Venises*, Paris, Gallimard, 1971

James Morris, *Venice*, London, Faber, 1964

Giovanni Musolini, *Santa Lucia e Venezia*,Venice, Stamperia di Venezia, 1987

Alfred de Musset, 'Le Fils du Titien', Paris, *Revue des Deux Mondes*, 15 March 1838

Alfred de Musset, *Contes d'Espagne et d'Italie*, Paris, Alphonse Lemerre, 1876

Les Noces de Cana de Véronèse. Une oeuvre et sa restauration, Paris, Editions de la Réunion des musées nationaux, 1992

John Julius Norwich, *History of Venice*, London, Allen Lane, 1982

Pier Maria Pasinetti, *Rosso veneziano*, 1959. English edition, *Venetian Red*, London, Secker and Warburg, 1960

Pier Maria Pasinetti, *Il Ponte dell'Accademia*, Milan, Bompiani, 1968

Pier Maria Pasinetti, *Dorsoduro*, Milan, Rizzoli, 1983

Pier Maria Pasinetti, *Piccole veneziane complicate*, Venice, Marsilio, 1996

Silvio Pellico, *Le Mie prigione*, Editore Bocca, 1832

Hugo Pratt, *Favola di Venezia*, Lizard, 1997

Marcel Proust, *A la recherche du temps perdu*, Paris, 1913–27. English edition, *Remembrance of Things Past*, 1922–31

Jean Raspail, *Vive Venise*, Editions Solar, 1992

Danilo Reato, *Maschere e travestimenti nella tradizione de carnevale di Venezia*, Venice, Arsenale Coperativa Editrice, 1995

Henri de Régnier, *L'Altana ou la Vie vénitienne*, Paris, Mercure de France, 1928

Henri de Régnier, *Esquisses vénitiennes*, Brussels, Editions Complexe, 1991

Rainer Maria Rilke, *Les Carnets de Malte Laurids Brigge*, Paris, Gallimard, 1991

Dorothea Ritter, *Venise. Photographies anciennes 1841–1920*, introduction by John Julius Norwich, Inter-Livres, 1994

Emmanuel Roblès, *Venise en hiver*, Paris, Editions du Seuil, 1981

Fulvio Roiter, *Vivre Venise*, text by Dominique Fernandez, Editions Mengès, 1978

Giandomenico Romanelli, *Tintoretto, La Scuola Grande di San Rocco*, Milan, Electa, 1995

Jean Roudaut, *Trois villes orientées*, Paris, Gallimard, 1967

John Ruskin, *Stones of Venice*, London, George Allen, 1886

Henri Sacchi, *La Dogaresse*, Paris, Editions du Seuil, 1994

Lisa Saint Aubin de Terán, with Michael Lindberg, *Venice, The Four Seasons*, London, Pavilion Books, 1996

George Sand, *Lettres d'un voyageur*, Paris, Félix Bonnaire, 1837

Marcel Schneider, *La Fin du carnaval*, Paris, Grasset, 1987

Vittorio Sgarbi, *Carpaccio*, Paris, Editions Liana Levi, 1994

Philippe Sollers, *Le Coeur absolu*, Paris, Gallimard, 1987

Philippe Sollers, *La Fête à Venise*, Paris, Gallimard, 1991

Bibliography

Philippe Sollers, *Venise éternelle. Les voyageurs photographes au siècle dernier*, Paris, J.C. Lattès, 1993

Mme de Staël, *Corinne ou l'Italie*, Paris, Gallimard, 1985

Adrian Stokes, *Critical Writings*, in particular *Venice, The Quattro Cento, Stones of Rimini* and *Colour and Form*, London, Thames & Hudson, 1996

André Suarès, *Voyage du Condottiere*, Granit, 1985

Hippolyte Taine, *Voyage en Italie*, Paris, Hachette, 1866

Jean Thuillier, *Campo Morto*, Paris, José Corti, 1992

Michel Tournier, *Les Météores*, Paris, Gallimard, 1975

Mark Twain, *The Innocents Abroad*, 1869

Diego Valeri, *Fantasia veneziana*, Padua, Le Tre Venezia, 1944

Diego Valeri, *Guida sentimentale di Venezia*, Florence, Sansoni, 1955

Jean-Louis Vaudoyer, *Les Délices de l'Italie*, Paris, Librairie Plon, 1924

Elisabeth Vedrenne, 'Scarpa-Venini. L'architecte et l'alchimiste', *L'oeil*, no 486, June 1997

Venise 360°, photographs by Attilio Boccazzi-Varotto, text by Francesco Valcanover, Priuli & Verlucca, Editori, Ivrea, 1991

Venise au siècle de Titien, Editions de la Réunion des Musées nationaux, 1993

Camille Villeneuve, *Deux mois en Italie, souvenirs et impressions d'une jeune fille*, 1885

Frédéric Vitoux, *L'Art de vivre à Venise*, photographs by Jérome Darblay, Paris, Flammarion, 1900

Richard Wagner, *My Life*, 1865-1880

A.M. Zanetti, *Della pittura veneziana*, 1771

Israel Zangwill, *Dreamers of the Ghetto*, London, Heinemann, 1898

Michel Zévaco, *Le Pont des Soupirs*, Paris, Librairie Arthème Fayard, 1948

Michel Zévaco, *Les Amants de Venise*, Paris, Librairie Arthème Fayard, 1950

Alvise Zorzi, *Venezia scomparsa*, Milan, Electa 1984
Alvise Zorzi, *Canale grande 'la piu bella strada del mundo'*, Milan, Rizzoli, 1991

Books on colour

Manlio Brusatin, *Storia dei colori*, Turin, Einaudi, 1986
Lodovico Dolce, *Dialogo della Pittura: intitiolata L' Aretino*, 1557. English edition *Aretin: A Dialogue on Painting*, 1770
Les femmes blondes selon les peintres de l'école de Venise, by two Venetians, Paris, A. Aubry, 1895
Remy de Gourmont, *Couleurs*, Brussels, Editions de la Chimère, 1923
Johannes Itten, *Art de la couleur*, Paris, Dessain & Tolra, 1985
Jean-Philippe Lenclos and Dominique Lenclos, *Les Couleurs de l'Europe. Géographie de la couleur*, Paris, Le Moniteur, 1995
Michel Pastoureau, *Dictionnaire des couleurs de notre temps: Symbolique et société*, Paris, Editions Bonneton, 1992
Philippe Pinguet, *Monet et Venise*, Paris, Herscher, 1986
Hugo Pratt, *Conversation avec Eddy Devolder*, Gerpinne, Editions Tabdem, 1990
David Rosand, *Painting in Sixteenth-Century Venice*, New Haven, Yale University Press, 1977
David Rosand, *The Meaning of the Mark*, Lawrence, Kan. University of Kansas Press, 1988

∞ Name index ∞

Name index